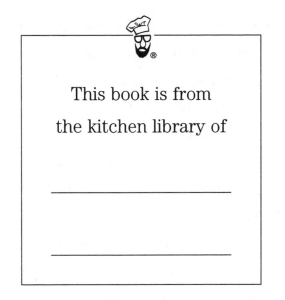

This book is from

the kitchen library of

_____

_____

ALSO BY ART GINSBURG, **Mr. Food®**

The **Mr. Food®** Cookbook, "OOH IT'S SO GOOD!!®" (1990)

Mr. Food® Cooks Like Mama (1992)

Mr. Food® Cooks Chicken (1993)

Mr. Food® Cooks Pasta (1993)

Mr. Food® Makes Dessert (1993)

Mr. Food® Cooks Real American (1994)

Mr. Food®'s Favorite Cookies (1994)

Mr. Food®'s Quick and Easy Side Dishes (1995)

Mr. Food® Grills It All in a Snap (1995)

Mr. Food®'s Fun Kitchen Tips and Shortcuts (and Recipes, Too!) (1995)

Mr. Food®'s Old World Cooking Made Easy (1995)

"Help, **Mr. Food®**! Company's Coming!" (1995)

Mr. Food®: Pizza 1-2-3 (1996)

Mr. Food® : Simply Chocolate (1996)

Mr. Food®

Meat
Around the Table

ART GINSBURG
Mr. Food®

WILLIAM MORROW AND COMPANY, INC.

NEW YORK

Library of Congress Cataloging-in-Publication Data

Ginsburg, Art.
    Mr. Food®: meat around the table / Art Ginsburg.
      p.   cm.
    Includes index.
    ISBN 0–688–14418–7
    1. Cookery (Meat).   I. Title.
    TX749.G52   1996   95–46434
    641.6'6—dc20   CIP

Printed in the United States of America

First Edition

1 2 3 4 5 6 7 8 9 10

BOOK DESIGN BY MICHAEL MENDELSOHN OF MM DESIGN 2000, INC.

Dedicated to

My dad, Charlie,

and my mom, Jennie,

who shaped my life and my food loves.

* * *

Dad was the best butcher I've ever known.

He taught me everything about meat, and am I ever grateful!

* * *

Mom showed me how to make everything Dad brought home into

wonderful dishes for us all to share.

* * *

Together they taught me the importance of family, tradition, and

hard work, and from them I learned the true meaning of

"OOH IT'S SO GOOD!!™"

Acknowledgments

★ ★ ★

Where to begin? I guess by thanking all my viewers and cookbook fans for all your requests for meat recipes, and also for the family favorites that you've graciously shared with me over the years. And for bringing together these meaty favorites, I've got to thank my **prime** team, led by Howard Rosenthal and Caryl Ginsburg Fantel. These two continue to **cut through the fat** and help me make the **grade** for you.

Joe Peppi, Patty Rosenthal, Janice Bruce, Alice Palombo, and Mike Arnaud are the folks who work with me to develop, test, and retest my recipes while Laura Ratcliff makes sense of it all for them and for me. Thanks, guys. You are truly a **cut** above! And along with them, I know I can **lean** on my administrative and sales team of Steve and Chuck Ginsburg, Tom Palombo, Marilyn Ruderman, Beth Ives, Stacey Dempsey, and Ethel and Carol Ginsburg.

Creating a **trim,** well-rounded cookbook takes input from many directions. I depend upon the special **seasoning** offered by Al Marchioni, Zachary Schisgal, Richard Aquan, Skip Dye, Deborah Weiss Geline, and the others at William Morrow, as well as the **saucy** contributions of Michael Mendelsohn and Roy Fantel.

For planning and preparing the menu, and serving up the finished dish, I have to thank my agent, Bill Adler, and my publicist, Phyllis Heller. I could certainly say that these two **marinate** and **garnish** my ideas so expertly.

Thanks again, everyone, for a job **well done**!

There are countless hardworking butchers and others in the meat industry today who deserve the thanks of us meat lovers, along with the generous companies and organizations who provide me with valuable information and products, including:

American Lamb Council

Beef Board Test Kitchens

Beef Industry Council of the Meat Board

Kansas Beef Council

National Pork Board

Pork Industry Group of the Meat Board

The U.S. Department of Agriculture Food Safety and
Inspection Service

Contents

* * *

Introduction

* * *

I'm so excited! Over the years I've shared so many recipes in my cookbooks... and on so many different subjects. But now I finally get to share a book totally devoted to one of my favorite food types: meat!

Don't take that the wrong way—I love chicken, pasta, and desserts, too, but there is something special and homey about meat. I think I know where that comes from, too—at least for me. It goes back to my dad. He was a butcher. And as a kid, I loved helping him with his work—any way I could. Every day Dad brought home a different cut of meat for Mom to cook up for dinner. And boy, was she good! Since she usually didn't know what he was going to bring, she would be ready to add a little of this and a little of that... and get a super meal on the table every night.

Mom often mixed up spices and rubbed them into the meat before cooking. Or, if she had extra time, she'd marinate it. There's nothing like marinated meat—that's why I knew I had to include a chapter on marinades, rubs, and sauces.

On special days Dad would bring home select meat cuts, like the ones in the chapter devoted to steaks, chops, and ribs. Boy, were they ever a hit! Other nights we might have had simple stews and one-pots (Mom loved them 'cause they were so easy). I mean, they take so little time to prepare—and cleanup is a breeze!

Of course, with Dad being in the meat business, we also had more than our share of ground meats. It's always been considered versatile, but I bet I still haven't been able to duplicate every ground meat dish that Mom made. There were so many... and we loved them all!

For a change of pace, Mom would cook our whole meal on top of the stove. Those were my earliest stovetop favorites, the first of many to follow. Oh, what Mom could concoct in her skillet! That was more than a few years ago, so with today's abundance of meat and vegetable choices, we can do some pretty amazing stovetop cooking, too. Let my chapter get you started.

At least once a week when we walked into our house we'd be greeted by the unmistakable, rich smell of something roasting in the oven. Sometimes Mom made things that cooked all day that were really worth the wait, and other times she made some pretty-quick-cookers, like the ones in Oven Easies.

And after we savored Mom's great roasts for dinner (there were so many different types—and Mom said they were the easiest kind of cooking), we could always count on having leftovers for soup, salad, or sandwiches. After you check out my recipes for these, you're going to want to make them even when you don't have left-overs! (Sure, you can almost always start with raw meat if you don't have any leftovers on hand.)

So, my hat is off to my mom and dad for the love they shared with me and my sister. I especially remember the warm times when we would "meat" around the table for our family meals. They certainly were the beginning of so much "OOH IT'S SO GOOD!!™" I wish the same for you and your family. Enjoy!

Charts and Information

* * *

From Supermarket to Super Meals: Playing It Safe

Stop! Before we go any further and really get into the fun and tasty parts of this book, I want to share some pointers that will help you and your family prepare and eat meat safely:

Safe Shopping

- Shop for meats and other perishables last so they don't sit in your shopping cart unrefrigerated for too long.
- Check the freshness dates on the packages. Do *not* buy items that are past the expiration ("sell by") date!
- Check the temperature of the meat case. If there is a thermometer, be sure it reads 40°F. or below.
- Wrap meats in plastic bags so any juices won't drip on other foods.
- If buying frozen meats, be sure that they are absolutely frozen solid.
- It's a good idea, especially in warm weather, to keep a cooler or ice chest in your car for transporting meats and other perishables home from the store. Whether going directly home or not, you must get the meat under refrigeration (or wrapped and into the freezer) immediately.

Safe Storage

- Always keep meats well chilled. That means below 40°F. in the refrigerator. Food-borne bacteria don't grow well in excessive cold (or heat). Use an inexpensive refrigerator thermometer (see page xxvi) to make sure your refrigerator temperature always remains between 35°F. and 40°F. and your freezer is kept at 0°F. or below.
- Never leave perishable prepared food at room temperature for more than 2 hours. This means a total of 2 hours during its life-time, and doesn't mean 2 hours every time you take it out of the refrigerator.
- Don't pack your refrigerator and freezer too tightly. Air needs to circulate around the stored items.
- Before freezing, wrap foods in aluminum foil and/or sealed plastic freezer bags. This not only protects the food but eliminates the possibility of contamination and keeps your refrigerator and freezer clean.
- Refrigerated ground meats should be used within 2 days, and other meats within 4 days, of purchase. And if you can't remember how long you've had them, play it safe and throw them out!

Safe Preparation

- Wash your hands, countertops, cutting boards, and utensils well with hot soapy water and rinse thoroughly before touching food. (Kitchen sponges and dishcloths should also be washed and changed daily, and certainly before and after coming in contact with raw meats.)
- Do not allow raw meat or meat juices to touch any foods that will not be cooked at high temperatures.
- Thaw food properly, either in the refrigerator, on a defrosting tray, or in the microwave according to the manufacturer's instructions. Only thaw food that you plan to cook right away.
- Always cover and refrigerate foods while marinating.

- Always discard any food or excess marinade that has come in contact with raw meat. If you are planning to use it with or on cooked meat, marinade that has come in contact with raw meat must first be brought to a full boil for at least 1 minute.
- **Never taste or eat any raw meat**—not even your meat loaf mixtures.
- Don't "double dip." If you use a cooking spoon to taste your food, wash it before using it again, or use a fresh spoon.
- Use a "quick-read" or "instant-read" thermometer to take the guesswork out of cooking meats. See pages xxi to xxv for charts on cooking meats and testing them for doneness.
- Do *not* partially cook foods, then store them or set them aside to finish cooking at a later time.
- Steaks and roasts should be cooked until the surfaces are well browned and they are at least medium-rare (145°F.) inside. All other meats should be cooked to an internal temperature of at least 140°F. to ensure elimination of any bacteria that may exist.
- **According to the U.S. Department of Agriculture, it is no longer acceptable to eat ground meat cooked to any doneness but well-done. Ground meats must be cooked until absolutely no pink remains and the juices run clear. This should eliminate your chances of coming in contact with any harmful bacteria.**

Safe Serving

- **Always put cooked foods on a clean (not just wiped!) platter. Never place cooked food on the same platter used for raw food unless the platter is completely washed first.**
- Serve food in small bowls instead of big ones. This allows you to keep the remainder of the cold food under refrigeration and the rest of the hot food in the oven, not sitting out.
- If serving a buffet, keep the cold foods cold and the hot foods hot.

Safe Traveling

- Always carry lunches to school or work in an insulated bag or box containing a cold pack.
- Wrap food well. Leaking juices are messy and unhealthy.
- Picnic with an ice chest or two. These shouldn't be constantly opened and closed, so it might work better for you to take two—one for beverages and snacks and another for mealtime foods.

Safe Leftovers

- Place leftovers in the refrigerator immediately. Do not let them cool to room temperature before refrigerating. Also, when you take restaurant food home in a doggie bag, be sure to get it under refrigeration immediately. So if, for example, you're planning to go right to the movies after dinner, don't take your leftovers!
- Don't let leftovers linger in the refrigerator before freezing! Eat or freeze them right away. It's a shame to have to throw them out—and it's so handy to have them available in the freezer!
- While reheating food, stir it frequently so that it heats evenly and is steaming hot throughout.
- My best rule for leftovers is "When in doubt, throw it out!"

What's What in the Meat Case

Since my father was a butcher, I grew up learning all about different cuts of meat and their best uses. But most people aren't that fortunate. Most people are intimidated by all the different choices and cuts that are displayed in our supermarket and meat market cases. (Thought you were the only one? Surprise! You're not alone!)

Today's meat counters sure have more to offer than ever before. Large cuts like whole beef ribs, hams, and legs of lamb are readily available, as well as smaller cuts like chops and steaks, and stew meats and ground meat products. Many markets sell soup bones as well as trimmed fat (for a multitude of uses, including for making sausage).

Sometimes you can purchase a side of beef or half a side, which is usually a very good value as long as you can store it properly until needed. (It also offers lots of varieties of cuts for different uses.) Buying in bulk often offers real savings, but don't be fooled. A bigger package doesn't always mean lower cost per pound.

Here's a list of tender, semi-tender, and less-tender meat cuts. Keep in mind that with proper cooking, a less tender meat cut can produce a very tender dish, while on the other hand, I've seen tender cuts that have turned out dry and tough from overcooking. A good rule to go by is that most tender cuts are best cooked with dry heat and less tender cuts are best prepared with moist heat. This can simply be a starting point for you—a guide. You can always ask your butcher for recommendations when you're unsure of what to buy for what purpose.

And remember, there are no rules. Experiment and make what you and your family like. But with this head start you're going to be able to sit back and take all the credit when your family bites into that tender meat!

Beef

Beef comes from mature steers and is recognized by its bright red meat with white exterior fat. Its flavor comes from the marbling of the fat, so obviously that varies with each cut, depending upon the differing amounts of fat in it.

Tender cuts: Most of the tender beef cuts come from the rib, the loin (short loin), and the sirloin. These are super grilled, broiled, roasted, panfried, or fancied up as in the steaks, chops, and ribs chapter. Familiar cuts include: Standing rib roast, rib eye roast, rib eye steaks, Delmonico, strip steaks, T-bone, porterhouse, tenderloin, filet mignon, and sirloin steaks.

Less-tender cuts: The less-tender beef cuts are usually from the chuck, the brisket, the short plate, the flank, and the round. These are usually less expensive but can be slow-cooked or marinated so that they'll be tender enough to practically melt in your mouth, just like the cuts that start out tender. The blade and bottom round steaks are best when cooked in a little liquid, braising them and making them tender as can be, too. Familiar cuts include: Chuck roast, short ribs, stew meat, ground beef, brisket, rump roast, round steaks, bottom round steaks, flank, eye of the round, cubed steaks, and top round.

Veal

Veal comes from young calves (usually less than 4 months old) and is recognized by its very light pink meat with minimal white exterior fat. It is firm, velvety meat with a mild flavor. Veal is quite versatile and especially popular in Italian and French cooking.

Tender cuts: These familiar cuts come from the rib, loin, sirloin, and leg: Loin chops, rolled loin roast, crown roast, rib chops, sirloin chops, and veal scallop.

Less-tender cuts: These familiar cuts come from the shoulder, neck, arm, shank, breast, heel of round, and rump: Veal neck, shoulder veal chops, veal breast, ground veal, veal stew, osso buco, veal cubed steak, and riblets.

Lamb

Lamb comes from young sheep (between 6 months and 1 year old). (Mutton is from older, mature sheep up to 2 years old.) It is recognized by its firm, moist, pale pink meat and mild flavor. Lamb has softer bones than beef and veal and can be cooked in a variety of ways.

Tender cuts: These familiar cuts come from the rib, loin, and hind legs: Rib chops, loin chops, crown rack, center cut leg, cubes for kebabs, sirloin roast, and sirloin chops.

Less-tender cuts: These familiar cuts come from the neck, shoulder, breast, forelegs, and shank: Neck slices, blade chops, lamb stew meat, ground lamb, rolled breast, spareribs, riblets, and lamb shanks.

Pork

Pork comes from the domesticated pig, a descendant of the wild boar. It is recognized by its beige to pink meat with snow-white exterior fat. It is juicy if cooked to an internal temperature of 160°F., but dry if overcooked. Pork is generally a lean meat with little marbling. It can be cooked dry or moist and is also good cured and dried.

Tender cuts: These familiar cuts come from the loin: Pork chops, pork roast, crown roast, tenderloin, loin roast, sirloin roast, country-style ribs, and Canadian bacon.

Less-tender cuts: These familiar cuts come from the shoulder (Boston butt), arm, leg, and side: Roasts and steaks, picnic roast, fresh or smoked ham, pigs' feet, cubes for kebabs, ground pork, spareribs, and slab bacon.

I know we grew up eating pork only cooked to well-done, but the Pork Industry Group and the National Pork Board recommend that today's pork be cooked to a final internal temperature of 160°F. to 170°F. (medium to well-done). Pork cooked to 160°F. will be faintly pink in the center. Bone-in cuts will have a slightly more intense pink color near the bone, but are perfectly safe to eat. Pork cooked to 170°F. (well-done) will lose almost all of its pink color and some additional juiciness, though it will be more flavorful.

Reading the Labels

Understanding how to read all types of food labels is important. I've got the scoop on meat labels. Here's what it all means:

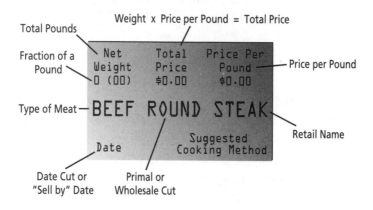

Meat packages must now also contain handling instructions. Please be sure to read and follow them carefully. Some labels give additional information about the meat, such as the grade and whether or not it has been previously frozen.

Check to see if the meat has bones or is boneless. Beware of labels placed over or hiding bones or fatty parts. And don't be afraid to ask the butcher or the supermarket meat manager for specific cuts or package sizes.

Timetable for Roasting Beef

To roast beef: Place beef roast, straight from the refrigerator, fat side up (if present), on a rack in a shallow roasting pan. Rub with herbs or season, if desired. Insert a meat thermometer into the center of the roast, not touching bone or fat. Always roast without a cover or the addition of liquid; otherwise, the meat will be braised. Remove the roast from the oven when a meat thermometer registers 10°F. below the desired doneness; the roast will continue to cook after removal from the oven. Allowing the roast to stand for 15 to 20 minutes after roasting makes carving easier.

Cut	Approximate Weight (in pounds)	Oven Temperature (in degrees F.)	Final Meat Thermometer Reading (in degrees F.)	Approximate Cooking Time* (minutes per pound)
Beef Rib Roast	8 to 10	300 to 325	140 (rare) 160 (medium)	19 to 21 23 to 25
Beef Rib Eye Roast	8 to 10	350	140 (rare) 160 (medium)	13 to 15 16 to 18
Beef Tenderloin Roast, Whole	4 to 6	425	140 (rare)	45 to 60 (total cooking time)
Beef Round Tip Roast	8 to 10	300 to 325	140 (rare) 160 (medium)	18 to 22 23 to 25
Beef Top Round Roast	6 to 10	300 to 325	140 (rare) 160 (medium)	17 to 19 22 to 24
Beef Top Loin Roast	7 to 9	300 to 325	140 (rare) 160 (medium)	9 to 11 13 to 15

*Cooking times are based on meat taken directly from the refrigerator.
Courtesy of the Meat Board Test Kitchens

Timetable for Roasting Veal

Roasting is the simplest and the most appropriate cooking method for larger cuts of veal from the loin, sirloin, and rib. A boneless veal shoulder arm, eye round, or rump roast also can be roasted successfully in a slow oven (300°F. to 325°F.).

To roast veal: Place roast (straight from the refrigerator), fat side up (if present), on a rack in an open shallow roasting pan. Season before or after cooking. Insert a meat thermometer into the thickest part of the roast, not touching bone or fat. Do not add water. Do not cover. Roast in a slow oven (300°F.) until a meat thermometer registers 5°F. below the desired doneness; the roast will continue to cook after removal from the oven. Allowing the roast to stand for 15 to 20 minutes after roasting makes carving easier.

Roasting at 300°F. to 325°F.

Cut	Approximate Weight (in pounds)	Final Meat Thermometer Reading (in degrees F.)	Approximate Cooking Time* (minutes per pound)
Loin	3 to 4	160 (medium)	34 to 36
		170 (well)	38 to 40
Loin (boneless)	2 to 3	160 (medium)	18 to 20
		170 (well)	22 to 24
Rib	4 to 5	160 (medium)	25 to 27
		170 (well)	29 to 31
Crown (12 to 14 ribs)	7½ to 9½	160 (medium)	19 to 21
		170 (well)	21 to 23
Rib Eye	2 to 3	160 (medium)	26 to 28
		170 (well)	30 to 33
Rump (boneless)	2 to 3	160 (medium)	33 to 35
		170 (well)	37 to 40
Shoulder (boneless)	2½ to 3	160 (medium)	31 to 34
		170 (well)	34 to 37

*Cooking times are based on meat taken directly from the refrigerator.
Courtesy of the Beef Board and Veal Committee of the Beef Industry Council

Timetable for Roasting Lamb

To roast lamb: Place lamb, fat side up, on a rack in an open roasting pan. Insert a meat thermometer into the center of the roast, not touching bone or fat. Do not add water. Do not cover. Roast in a slow oven (300°F. to 325°F.) until cooked to desired doneness. Season with salt and pepper, if desired.

Roasting at 300°F. to 325°F.

Cut	Approximate Weight (in pounds)	Final Meat Thermometer Reading (in degrees F.)	Approximate Cooking Time* (minutes per pound)
Leg	7 to 9	140 (rare)	15 to 20
		160 (medium)	20 to 25
		170 (well)	25 to 30
Leg	5 to 7	140 (rare)	20 to 25
		160 (medium)	25 to 30
		170 (well)	30 to 35
Leg (boneless)	4 to 7	140 (rare)	25 to 30
		160 (medium)	30 to 35
		170 (well)	35 to 40
Leg, Shank Half	3 to 4	140 (rare)	30 to 35
		160 (medium)	40 to 45
		170 (well)	45 to 50
Leg, Sirloin Half	3 to 4	140 (rare)	25 to 30
		160 (medium)	35 to 40
		170 (well)	45 to 50
Shoulder† (boneless)	3½ to 5	140 (rare)	30 to 35
		160 (medium)	35 to 40
		170 (well)	40 to 45

*Cooking times are based on meat taken directly from the refrigerator.
†For presliced, bone-in shoulder, add 5 minutes per pound to times recommended for boneless shoulder.
Courtesy of the Lamb Committee of the National Live Stock and Meat Board

Timetable for Roasting Pork

To roast pork: Place pork, fat side up, on a rack in an open roasting pan. Rub with herbs or season, if desired. Insert a meat thermometer into the center of the roast, not touching bone or fat. Do not add water. Do not cover. Roast in a slow oven (300°F. to 325°F.), unless instructed otherwise, to 5°F. below the recommended degree of doneness; the roast will continue to cook after removal from the oven. Allowing the roast to stand for 15 to 20 minutes after roasting makes carving easier.

Cut	Approximate Weight (in pounds)	Oven Temperature (in degrees F.)	Final Meat Thermometer Reading (in degrees F.)	Approximate Cooking Time* (minutes per pound)
Loin, Center (bone in)	3 to 5	325	160 (medium) 170 (well)	20 to 25 26 to 31
Blade Loin/Sirloin (boneless, tied)	2½ to 3	325	170 (well)	33 to 38
Boneless Rib End— Chef's Prime	2 to 4	325	160 (medium) 170 (well)	26 to 31 28 to 33
Top (double)	3 to 4	325	160 (medium) 170 (well)	29 to 34 33 to 38
Top	2 to 4	325	160 (medium) 170 (well)	23 to 33 30 to 40
Crown	6 to 10	325	170 (well)	20 to 25

Cut	Approximate Weight (in pounds)	Oven Temperature (in degrees F.)	Final Meat Thermometer Reading (in degrees F.)	Approximate Cooking Time* (minutes per pound)
Leg				
Whole (bone in)	12	325	170 (well)	23 to 25
Top (inside)	3½	325	170 (well)	38 to 42
Bottom (outside)	3½	325	170 (well)	40 to 45
Blade Boston (boneless)	3 to 4	325	170 (well)	40 to 45
Tender-loin	½ to 1 pound	425	160 (medium) 170 (well)	27 to 29 30 to 32
Backribs		425	tender	1½ to 1¾ hours total cooking time
Country-Style Ribs	1-inch slices	425	tender	1½ to 1¾ hours total cooking time
Spareribs		425	tender	1½ to 1¾ hours total cooking time

˙Cooking times are based on meat taken directly from the refrigerator.

Courtesy of the Meat Board Test Kitchens and Pork Industry Group

Thermometers Are on the Rise

I used to think that thermometers were an unnecessary kitchen tool—just an extra cooking step. Well, let me tell you that once I found out how really easy they are to use, and how helpful they are, I changed my mind. Thermometers take a lot of the guesswork out of cooking, so they can make us look like kitchen heroes with no fuss at all! There are a few different types of thermometers, so let me share a few tips on what to look for:

- **Oven thermometers** are meant to hang over an oven rack and show the temperature of an oven. If the temperature registered on your oven thermometer doesn't match your oven setting, you should adjust your oven setting accordingly until the oven gets to the desired temperature. If that happens on a regular basis, you should have your oven calibration checked by a professional who can make any necessary internal adjustments.
- **Quick-Read or Instant-Read thermometers** are used to check the internal temperature of many foods, especially meats. You just have to insert the probe into the center of the meat without touching any fat or bone. Within a few seconds you'll have an accurate reading of the internal meat temperature. **These are not to be used in the oven or the microwave.**
- **Refrigerator thermometers** can help us keep our refrigerators at just the right temperature to be both safe *and* fuel-efficient. They are hung over a refrigerator rack and can be kept there permanently, to help you prolong the shelf life of your foods.
- **Meat thermometers** are the ones that we insert into a roast before cooking; they stay in the meat while it cooks and usually indicate the doneness of beef, veal, lamb, and pork by the inter-

ALWAYS COOK
GROUND MEAT UNTIL
WELL-DONE
NO PINK REMAINS AND
THE JUICES RUN CLEAR

nal temperature. The biggest drawback of these is that because they are kept in the meat during cooking, they allow juices to escape all during that time.

Whichever thermometers you choose, be sure they are well made and easy to read. An inaccurate thermometer is useless.

Meat Carving Tips

How could I write a book about meat and not include the basics of carving? Since this book includes beef, veal, lamb, and pork, and each cut of meat has its own unique carving techniques, I'm going to give you a few general pointers that you can apply to any roasts. Don't worry—I won't get too technical! Carving simply means slicing a roast, steak, or other meat cut into serving-sized pieces. It's really easy to do if you have the proper tools.

- Make sure that your meat is cooked to the proper doneness. If it's too rare, it will be difficult to carve. And if it's overcooked, it might be tough, or too tender, making it fall apart when you try to cut it.
- Let a roast sit out of the oven in the roasting pan for 10 to 15 minutes after cooking, so that the cooking process can finish.
- Place the item to be carved on a clean cutting board that's bigger than the item. Be sure it is sitting solidly on the board and not wobbling. Cutting boards with a well, or a ridged edge, work great for roasts since they collect the juices that run off during carving. I also prefer boards without prongs; that way the meat can be moved as you carve each slice.
- Use a sharp knife with an 8- to 10-inch blade for carving roasts, and a knife with a smaller blade for cutting steaks. It's important to keep your knives sharp, and there's such a variety of knife sharpeners available today that it's not hard to do.
- A 2-pronged kitchen fork is helpful for holding the meat in position while carving, and also for removing the sliced meat from the

board. The fork should not be repeatedly inserted into the meat, however, because piercing it allows the flavorful juices to escape.

- You can carve your meat either in the kitchen or at the dining table, but wherever it's done, make sure that you have enough room to maneuver. Also, have your serving platter handy so that you've got a place to put the carved slices.
- Cut along the bone first, then carve toward the bone of roasts, making sure your knife is level; that's how you cut even slices.
- Cut larger roasts and steaks across the grain (see Note) with your knife blade at a slight angle. This will give you larger, more tender slices.
- If your roast is held together with string or skewers, remove them carefully as you carve. This helps keep the meat from falling apart.
- You may want to carve just the amount of meat that you'll need for your meal. If you leave the rest of it whole, it'll stay moister for the next time you serve it.
- Before serving, spoon or pour any pan drippings or sauce over the carved meats... and enjoy!

NOTE: What does "cut across the grain" mean, anyway? Throughout this book I often suggest cutting steaks and roasts "across the grain." What that really refers to is the direction the meat should be carved in relation to the direction of the fibers of the meat. The fibers generally run through the meat all in the same direction, except in certain cuts like brisket, where the grains change directions. Watch out for that as you carve. See the illustration below.

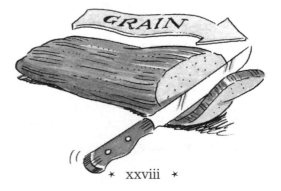

The Lighter Side of Meat

Beef, veal, lamb, and pork have a reputation for being hearty main dishes. But hearty doesn't have to mean heavy. Meat can be the perfect solution for those of us watching what we eat. Unless we're under a physician's care or on a special meatless diet, meat should be a part of all our diets.* Sure, because it's packed with protein! When it's prepared using my easy tips, and eaten in moderation, you'll get to enjoy the lighter side of meat as never before:

- Choose lean cuts of meat and trim away any visible fat before preparing. With ground meats, select leaner blends, preferably ones that have a 90/10 meat to fat ratio (see page 66).
- Serve moderate-sized portions, like 3 to 4 ounces of cooked meat (weighing approximately 4 to 6 ounces raw) per adult. (That would be about the size of a deck of playing cards.)
- Choose cooking methods (like roasting, broiling, grilling, and baking on a rack) that allow fat to drip away during cooking. When sautéing, use nonstick pans and nonstick vegetable spray or a bit of butter or oil.

> ### FOR A LEANER FINISHED DISH,
> ### TRIM EXCESS FAT BEFORE COOKING

- Remove the layer of fat that rises to the top of stews, roasts, and soups. Chilling makes this a breeze, so it's even easier to do with dishes that are made ahead, chilled, and reheated. Or, you can simply add a few ice cubes to the cooked dish. As soon as the fat sticks to them, remove the ice cubes from the cooking pan.

*Always consult your physician when you have any questions about your diet.

- Drain off the fat after browning ground meats or larger meat cuts and before adding any other ingredients.
- For a light meaty alternative, try stir-frying strips of meat with fresh vegetables.
- Soups, salads, and sandwiches can be a super way to enjoy the flavors of your favorite meats while extending them with vegetables, beans, pastas, rice, and/or broth.

Notes from **Mr. Food**®

* * *

Serving Sizes

I like to serve generous portions myself, so I generally figure that way when I list the number of portions to expect from my recipes. Yes, appetites do vary and *you* know the special food loves of your eaters, so, as always, you be the judge of how much to make.

Packaged Foods

Packaged food sizes may vary by brand. Generally, the sizes indicated in these recipes are average sizes. If you can't find the exact package size listed in the ingredients, whatever package is closest in size will usually do the trick.

Rubs, Marinades, and Sauces

It's time to get out our spices, our mixing bowls and spoons, and start preparing our favorite meat dishes. And what better way to start than by mixing up a rub, marinade, or sauce?!

The best part about the recipes that follow is their versatility. The rubs can be used on beef, veal, lamb, or pork—and on anything from roasts to steaks and chops, and even mixed into ground meats. Not only are the marinades great flavor boosters, but they're the perfect solution to help tenderize less-tender meat cuts. And the sauces. . . just team them with your favorite meat dishes to add a whole new taste that your gang is sure to love. (And I bet they'll love *you* for making these, too!)

Rubs, Marinades, and Sauces

Sauces

Back-to-Basics Brown Gravy 13
Sherry Mushroom Sauce 14
Shortcut Béarnaise Sauce 14
Tomato Red Relish 15
Horseradish Sauce 16
Lemon Relish 16

Tips and Instructions for Rubs

For each rub recipe included here, the instructions are as follows:

- Combine all the ingredients in a plastic container with a tight-fitting lid; mix well, then spread onto or rub into meat anytime from 5 hours before cooking right up to just before cooking. Cook meat as desired. If not using right away, except for those recipes that require refrigeration (as noted), store the rub in an airtight container in a cool, dry place until ready to use. For recipes that require refrigeration, mix as above, cover, and chill until ready to use.
- **Discard leftover rubs that have come in contact with raw meat.**

Mustard Rub

* * *

²/₃ cup

½ cup Dijon-style mustard
¼ cup dried parsley flakes
2 tablespoons dried orange or lemon peel
2 tablespoons dried rosemary
1 tablespoon cracked black pepper

See above for mixing instructions.

NOTE: Cover and refrigerate any unused rub for future use.

Spicy Seasoning Rub

* * *

³/₄ cup

¹/₂ cup chili powder
¹/₄ cup ground cumin
2 tablespoons garlic powder
1 tablespoon dried oregano
1 to 2 teaspoons cayenne pepper (to taste)

See page 5 for mixing instructions.

Pepper-Herb Rub

* * *

²/₃ cup

¹/₃ cup dried basil
¹/₄ cup lemon-pepper seasoning
2 tablespoons onion powder
¹/₄ cup ground sage

See page 5 for mixing instructions.

Garlic Mustard Rub

* * *

³/₄ cup

½ cup Creole or other spicy mustard
¼ cup dried minced onion
2 tablespoons dry Cajun seasoning blend
1½ tablespoons chopped fresh or bottled garlic
2 teaspoons hot pepper sauce

See page 5 for mixing instructions.

NOTE: Cover and refrigerate any unused rub for future use.

Cajun Rub

* * *

½ cup

⅓ cup Cajun seasoning blend
2 tablespoons cracked black pepper
2 tablespoons fennel seed, crushed

See page 5 for mixing instructions.

Dry Barbecue Rub

* * *

1 cup

1 jar (2 ounces) hickory-smoked, mesquite barbecue, or mesquite grill
  seasoning
2 tablespoons garlic powder
2 tablespoons whole mustard seed
2 tablespoons cracked black pepper

See page 5 for mixing instructions.

Spicy Dry Rub

* * *

²/₃ cup

¼ cup mustard powder
3 tablespoons dried oregano
2 tablespoons chili powder
1 tablespoon garlic powder
1 tablespoon salt
1 tablespoon black pepper

See page 5 for mixing instructions.

Fiery Creole Pepper Rub

* * *

1/2 cup

3 tablespoons dried thyme

3 tablespoons paprika

2 teaspoons black pepper

2 teaspoons garlic powder

2 teaspoons onion powder

2 teaspoons cayenne pepper

2 teaspoons white pepper

2 teaspoons salt

See page 5 for mixing instructions.

Aztec Rub

* * *

1/2 cup

1/3 cup crushed cumin seed

1 1/2 tablespoons chopped fresh or bottled garlic

1 tablespoon liquid smoke

1 tablespoon kosher (coarse) salt

1 teaspoon cayenne pepper

1/2 cup olive oil

See page 5 for mixing instructions.

NOTE: Cover and refrigerate any unused rub for future use.

Tips and Instructions for Marinades

For each marinade recipe included here, the instructions are as follows:

- To make a marinade without oil, combine all the ingredients in a bowl; mix until well blended.
- To make a marinade with oil, combine all the ingredients except the oil in a food processor or blender. Gradually add the oil while processing. Transfer to a glass or plastic storage container, cover, and chill until ready to use. Unused marinades (those that have not come in contact with any raw meat or meat juices) should last for several weeks in your refrigerator.
- For flavor only, marinate meat for 30 minutes. Otherwise, for flavor and tenderizing, I recommend marinating meat for 5 to 12 hours or overnight. Do not overmarinate. That breaks down the meat fibers and results in a mushy texture.
- **Discard leftover marinades that have come in contact with raw meat.**

Frisco Marinade

* * *

2²/₃ cups

2 cups dry red wine
1 can (6 ounces) frozen orange juice concentrate, thawed
3 tablespoons crushed dried rosemary
¹/₄ cup chopped fresh or bottled garlic
1 tablespoon mustard powder
2 teaspoons black pepper
2 teaspoons salt

See page 10 for mixing instructions.

Lemon-Garlic Marinade

* * *

1¹/₂ cups

1 cup olive oil
¹/₂ cup lemon juice
¹/₄ cup dried oregano
2 tablespoons chopped fresh or bottled garlic
1 tablespoon ground cumin
1 tablespoon black pepper
1 teaspoon salt

See page 10 for mixing instructions.

Teriyaki Marinade

* * *

About 2 cups

1 cup soy sauce
3/4 cup honey
2 teaspoons ground dried ginger
1 tablespoon chopped fresh or bottled garlic

See page 10 for mixing instructions.

Spicy Italian Marinade

* * *

1 cup

1 bottle (8 ounces) Italian dressing
4 teaspoons hot pepper sauce

See page 10 for mixing instructions.

Sauces

Back-to-Basics Brown Gravy

* * *

About 2 cups

2 tablespoons butter
2 tablespoons all-purpose flour
1 can (14½ ounces) ready-to-use beef broth
1 teaspoon browning and seasoning sauce

In a small saucepan, melt the butter over medium-low heat. Gradually add the flour, whisking for about 1 minute, until well blended and lightly browned. Remove from the heat, then gradually add the broth and the browning and seasoning sauce, stirring constantly. Bring to a boil over medium heat, then reduce the heat to low and simmer until smooth.

NOTE: Here are some options for things you can add along with the broth: For a richer, heartier gravy, add ¼ cup spaghetti sauce. Or, to add a simple touch of elegance, add ¼ cup dry red or white wine. And for flavor variation, you could add 1 teaspoon of dried thyme or rosemary or ground black pepper. Make it to suit your main course—and your favorite tastes!

Sherry Mushroom Sauce

* * *

1¼ cups

1 can (10 ounces) brown gravy
1 cup fresh mushrooms, thinly sliced (about 2 ounces)
½ teaspoon dried thyme
2 tablespoons cream sherry or sweet white wine
¼ teaspoon browning and seasoning sauce

In a small saucepan, combine all the ingredients. Heat over medium heat for 8 to 10 minutes, stirring occasionally.

Shortcut Béarnaise Sauce

* * *

1 cup

2 tablespoons white vinegar
1½ teaspoons ground dried tarragon
¼ teaspoon garlic powder
½ teaspoon chopped fresh parsley
1 cup mayonnaise

In a small saucepan, combine the vinegar, tarragon, garlic powder, and parsley; simmer over medium heat for 1 to 2 minutes, stirring occasionally. Place the mayonnaise in a small bowl and add the vinegar and spice mixture; blend until smooth and creamy.

NOTE: Serve over cooked beef or veal as the perfect fresh accent.

Tomato Red Relish

* * *

3 cups

4 or 5 large ripe tomatoes
1/4 cup chopped fresh basil
1 tablespoon sugar
3 tablespoons white vinegar
2 tablespoons finely chopped onion
1/2 teaspoon garlic powder
1/2 teaspoon salt

Cut the tomatoes in half crosswise, then squeeze gently to remove the juice and seeds; cut the tomatoes into cubes. Place the cubes in a medium-sized bowl and add the remaining ingredients; stir until well mixed. May serve immediately, or cover and chill for up to 1 week.

NOTE: I think this tastes best at room temperature, so if serving after being chilled, try letting it come to room temperature before using. (It should take 15 to 20 minutes.)

Horseradish Sauce

* * *

²/₃ cup

½ cup prepared horseradish, well drained
½ cup mayonnaise
1 teaspoon lemon juice
¼ teaspoon white pepper

In a small bowl, combine all the ingredients and mix well. Cover and chill for at least 30 minutes before serving.

Lemon Relish

* * *

1½ cups

½ of a small onion
1 lemon, quartered and seeded
½ cup sour cream
1 can (8 ounces) crushed pineapple, drained
2 tablespoons light brown sugar

Place the onion and lemon in the bowl of a food processor that is fitted with the cutting blade. Process on low speed for 10 seconds, or until the mixture is chunky. Add the remaining ingredients and process on low speed for 5 seconds, or until everything is blended, being careful not to liquefy the mixture.

NOTE: Serve with pot roast or any other beef dish, or almost anything from eggs to cooked chicken and fish.

Steaks, Chops, and Ribs

When you ask the gang what kind of meat they want for dinner, I bet they usually ask for thick steaks, juicy chops, or meaty ribs. These cuts are usually at the top of the list, so that's just why I put them together here. And, boy, do we have lots of choices for how to cook them!

We can broil, grill, or panfry these cuts. Check pages xvi to xix for specific information regarding which cuts are the most and least tender. Now I've got some tips that'll help you make the most of your steaks, chops, and ribs:

- If you have questions about which meat cut to use for what, don't be shy—ask your butcher.
- Steaks and chops should be at least 1 inch thick and will be even juicier when cut $1\frac{1}{2}$ to 2 inches thick. Remember, though, the thicker they are, the longer they'll take to cook.
- Several small slits on the outside edge of steaks will help prevent the edges from curling.

- Turn steaks, chops, and ribs with tongs. Piercing them while cooking, as happens when turning with a fork, releases the juices instead of keeping them inside.
- Don't overcook tender or semi-tender meat cuts. It makes them dry and tough.
- If cooking with a sauce or glaze, baste occasionally unless the recipe indicates otherwise. This will enhance the flavors and keep the meat moist.
- To test for doneness, cut a small slit in the center and check the color. For bone-in steaks, cut along the bone. For thicker steaks and chops, insert a meat thermometer into the thickest part, not touching fat or bone. See pages xxi to xxv for specific doneness information on beef, veal, lamb, and pork.

Steaks, Chops, and Ribs

Cajun Steak

* * *

3 to 4 servings

Cajun flavors are really popular all around the country, and they can be a hit in your home, too. I really mean in your backyard, 'cause this is a great grilling steak.

2 teaspoons salt
1 teaspoon black pepper
1/4 teaspoon cayenne pepper
1/4 teaspoon paprika
1/4 teaspoon garlic powder
One 2-pound boneless beef top sirloin steak

Preheat the broiler. In a small bowl, combine all of the ingredients except the steak; mix well. Rub the seasoning mix on each side of the steak. Place the steak on a broiler pan or rimmed cookie sheet that has been coated with nonstick vegetable spray. Broil for 7 to 8 minutes per side for medium-rare, or until desired doneness.

NOTE: If you want some really delicious sandwiches, slice this thin and layer it on crusty rolls.

THOROUGHLY WASH HANDS OR ANY ITEMS IMMEDIATELY AFTER CONTACT WITH RAW MEAT

Marinated Flank Steak

* * *

4 to 6 servings

To sauce or not to sauce (Sherry Mushroom Sauce, I mean)? Either way, it's a crowd-pleaser.

- ²/₃ cup vegetable oil
- ²/₃ cup dry red wine
- ¹/₄ cup pickling spice
- 1 tablespoon sugar
- 1 teaspoon whole black peppercorns
- 1 teaspoon salt
- 1 teaspoon lemon juice
- 1³/₄ to 2 pounds beef flank steak, about 1 inch thick

In a medium-sized bowl, combine all of the ingredients except the steak; whisk until well mixed. Pour half of the marinade mixture into a 9" × 13" baking dish; lay the steak in the marinade. Pour the remaining marinade over the steak. Cover and chill for 8 to 10 hours, or overnight, turning once. Preheat the broiler. Place the steak on a broiler pan or rimmed cookie sheet, discarding the marinade, and broil for 9 to 11 minutes per side for medium-rare, or until desired doneness. Cut the steak across the grain into thin slices and serve.

NOTE: The Sherry Mushroom Sauce I mentioned is on page 14. You can serve this plain or with the sauce. The sauce really seems to bring out the flavor of the marinated steak.

Apricot Glazed Steak

* * *

6 to 8 servings

If you thought that apricot preserves belong only on toast, look here. Their fruity taste broiled on beef is a winner, too. Let's make a "toast" to this new combo.

2 to 2½ pounds beef flank steak, about 1 inch thick
1 cup apricot preserves
2 teaspoons soy sauce
1½ teaspoons seasoned salt
1 teaspoon ground thyme
¼ teaspoon cayenne pepper

Preheat the broiler. Place the steak on a broiler pan or rimmed cookie sheet that has been lined with aluminum foil that has been coated with nonstick vegetable spray. In a medium-sized bowl, combine the remaining ingredients; mix well. Brush the steak generously with the sauce, reserving the remaining sauce. Broil for 8 to 10 minutes per side for medium, or until desired doneness, basting halfway through the cooking with the reserved sauce. Discard any remaining sauce. Slice across the grain into ¼-inch slices.

NOTE: You can use peach or pineapple preserves in place of apricot, if you prefer.

Double Melt-Away Steak

* * *

3 to 4 servings

This is so simple! The idea is to season butter and let it flavor your steak as it melts. And when the tender meat melts in your mouth, it's like having a double treat.

1/2 cup (1 stick) butter, slightly softened
1 tablespoon minced garlic
1/4 teaspoon lemon juice
2 teaspoons dried parsley flakes
One 1 1/2- to 2-pound beef porterhouse or T-bone steak, 2 inches thick
1/2 teaspoon onion powder
1/4 teaspoon salt

In a small bowl, combine the butter, garlic, lemon juice, and parsley flakes; mix well. Place down the center of a 12-inch square piece of waxed paper and roll into a 1-inch-thick log. Wrap tightly and refrigerate for about 2 hours, or until firm. Preheat the broiler. Sprinkle each side of the steak evenly with the onion powder and salt. Place the steak on a broiler pan or rimmed cookie sheet and broil for 7 to 9 minutes. Turn the steak over and place four 1/4-inch slices of the herbed butter on the top; broil for 7 to 9 more minutes for medium-rare, or until desired doneness. Remove the steak from the broiler and cut around the bone, removing the bone. Cut the steak across the grain into 1/4-inch slices. Top each serving with an additional 1/4-inch slice of butter and allow to melt. Save any unused herbed butter in the refrigerator for future use.

Sweet and Tangy Steak

* * *

2 to 3 servings

Here's an easy-to-make marinated steak that's bursting with flavor, and best of all, you can marinate it overnight. Then you'll be able to have dinner on the table in under 20 minutes.

1/2 cup steak sauce

1/4 cup firmly packed light brown sugar

1/4 cup lime juice

1 teaspoon crushed red pepper

1 to 1 1/2 pounds boneless beef loin strip steak, 1 inch thick

1 teaspoon cornstarch

In a small bowl, combine the steak sauce, brown sugar, lime juice, and red pepper; mix well. Set aside ½ cup of the sauce, covered, in the refrigerator, and place the rest in a resealable plastic storage bag with the steak; turn to coat. Close the bag securely, then marinate in the refrigerator for 6 to 8 hours or overnight, turning occasionally. Preheat the broiler. Place the steak on a broiler pan or rimmed cookie sheet that has been covered with aluminum foil that has been coated with nonstick vegetable spray, discarding the used marinade. Broil the steak for 14 to 16 minutes for medium-rare, or until desired doneness, turning halfway through the cooking. Meanwhile, add the cornstarch to the reserved sauce and whisk until dissolved. Bring to a boil over medium-high heat and boil, stirring constantly, for 3 to 4 minutes, until slightly thickened. When the steak is done, cut across the grain into thin slices and serve with the sauce.

NOTE: To create a whole new marinade, try using Caribbean-style and other interesting steak sauce flavors. They should be available in the international section of your supermarket.

Snappy Dijon Steak

* * *

6 to 8 servings

This broiled steak is truly a "snap," and the blend of the Dijon mustard and tarragon gives it such a zesty flavor! I'm sure you'll be making this again and again for your gang.

  1½ pounds beef top round or boneless top sirloin steak, about 1 inch
    thick
  2 tablespoons mayonnaise
  1 tablespoon Dijon-style mustard
  1 teaspoon dried tarragon
  ¼ teaspoon salt
  ¼ teaspoon black pepper

Preheat the broiler. Place the steak on a broiler pan or rimmed cookie sheet that has been coated with nonstick vegetable spray. In a small bowl, combine the remaining ingredients; mix well. Spread the mixture over the steak, coating well. Broil for 16 to 19 minutes for medium-rare, or to desired doneness beyond that, turning halfway through the cooking.

> FOR A LEANER FINISHED DISH,
> TRIM EXCESS FAT BEFORE COOKING

Cupboard Steak

* * *

4 servings

You're probably wondering why this is called "cupboard" steak. Well, that's easy...it's 'cause all the ingredients are found right in your kitchen cupboard.

- 1 cup chunky salsa
- ½ cup ketchup
- ¼ cup firmly packed light brown sugar
- 2 tablespoons Dijon-style mustard
- 4 beef eye of round steaks (4 to 6 ounces each), about ¾ inch thick

In a medium-sized bowl, combine the salsa, ketchup, brown sugar, and mustard; mix well. Place in a resealable plastic storage bag with the steaks; seal tightly and turn to completely coat the meat. Marinate in the refrigerator for 2 to 3 hours, turning occasionally. Preheat the broiler. Place the steaks on a broiler pan or rimmed cookie sheet that has been covered with aluminum foil and coated with nonstick vegetable spray, discarding the marinade. Broil the steak for 14 to 16 minutes for medium-rare, or until desired doneness, turning halfway through the cooking.

Asian Garlic Steak

* * *

4 to 6 servings

This sauce packs quite a punch. Team it with tender beef and you're on your way to an easy dinner that's sure to please.

1 tablespoon vegetable oil
1½ to 2 pounds beef flank or boneless top sirloin steak, 1 inch thick, cut into thin strips
⅓ cup soy sauce
1 cup sweet-and-sour (duck) sauce
2 tablespoons minced garlic
1 tablespoon ground ginger
½ teaspoon hot pepper sauce
½ teaspoon black pepper
1 bag (16 ounces) frozen stir-fry vegetable mix, thawed and drained

FOR A LEANER FINISHED DISH, TRIM EXCESS FAT BEFORE COOKING

In a large skillet, heat the oil over medium heat and brown the steak for 5 to 6 minutes per side. Meanwhile, in a small bowl, combine the remaining ingredients except the vegetables; mix well. Add to the steak, along with the vegetables. Reduce the heat to low and simmer for 3 to 5 more minutes, stirring until completely mixed and heated through.

NOTE: Serve over hot cooked brown or white rice. And with the wide variety of frozen vegetable mixes available, this recipe can be different every time you make it!

Blackened Sirloin Steak

* * *

4 to 6 servings

Here's a blackened steak that you can make at home with spices you have on hand. And there's no smoke-filled kitchen like with the true New Orleans version. What could be better or easier?

2 teaspoons paprika
1 teaspoon crushed dried thyme
1/2 teaspoon onion powder
1/2 teaspoon garlic powder
1/2 teaspoon salt
1/2 teaspoon sugar
1/4 teaspoon cayenne pepper
1/2 teaspoon black pepper
One 2 1/2-pound boneless beef top sirloin steak, 1 1/2 to 2 inches thick

In a small bowl, combine all the ingredients except the steak; mix well. Brush the steak with the seasoning mixture until completely coated. Heat a large nonstick skillet over high heat until hot. Carefully place the steak in the skillet and cook for 12 to 14 minutes for medium-rare, or until desired doneness and the coating is blackened, turning halfway through the cooking. Cut across the grain into thin slices and serve.

NOTE: This seasoning blend works on any type of meat, or even fish or chicken.

Country Grilled Steak

* * *

4 servings

Think you can't grill a coated steak? If seeing it doesn't make a believer out of you, tasting it will… and it's sure to become a family favorite!

- ½ cup yellow cornmeal
- 2 teaspoons chili powder
- ½ teaspoon salt
- ½ teaspoon black pepper
- 4 beef rib eye steaks (8 to 10 ounces each)

Preheat the grill to medium-high heat. In a medium-sized bowl, combine all the ingredients except the steaks; mix well. Dip each steak into the mixture and pat the coating firmly into the steak, covering completely. Grill the steaks for 10 to 12 minutes, or until desired doneness, turning them over once.

NOTE: This works just as well on an indoor grill or, if you prefer, in the broiler. But if you're broiling it, then, after you coat the steak, spray it with nonstick vegetable spray so that the coating will get crisp and brown.

KEEP RAW AND COOKED MEATS SEPARATED

Onion-Smothered Strip Steak

* * *

4 servings

Mmm—steak and onions. What could be better? I guess just steak and onions done in a flash (like this)!

¹/₄ cup vegetable oil
4 medium-sized onions, thinly sliced
1 teaspoon salt, divided
³/₄ teaspoon black pepper, divided
4 boneless beef loin strip steaks (8 ounces each)
¹/₂ teaspoon garlic powder

In a large skillet, heat the oil over medium-high heat and add the onions, ¹/₂ teaspoon salt, and ¹/₄ teaspoon pepper. Cook for 18 to 20 minutes, or until the onions are very tender and have begun to brown, stirring occasionally. Sprinkle the remaining salt and pepper and the garlic powder over the steaks on both sides and place on a rimmed cookie sheet. Broil for 7 to 9 minutes for medium-rare, or until desired doneness, turning halfway through the cooking. Cover the steak evenly with the onions and serve.

NOTE: Try this with your favorite cut of steak, or even beef or calf's liver. They all work!

Jamaican Jerk Steak

* * *

4 servings

Make a big batch of this to have on hand as a seasoning sprinkle for steaks, chops, and roasts when you want a quick taste of the tropics at your fingertips.

- ¼ cup garlic powder
- ¼ cup dried thyme
- ¼ cup ground ginger
- 2 tablespoons ground allspice
- 2 tablespoons ground cloves
- 2 tablespoons kosher (coarse) salt
- 2 teaspoons cayenne pepper
- 2 teaspoons black pepper
- One 1½- to 2-pound boneless beef top sirloin or top round steak, 1 inch thick
- 1 tablespoon vegetable oil

In a medium-sized bowl, combine all of the ingredients except the steak and oil; mix well. Remove 1 to 2 tablespoons of the seasoning mixture and press it into both sides of the steak. Reserve the remaining "Jerk" mixture in an airtight plastic container for future use. In a large skillet, heat the oil over medium-high heat and add the steak. Reduce the heat to medium and cook for 7 to 9 minutes, or until desired doneness, turning halfway through the cooking.

THOROUGHLY
WASH HANDS
OR ANY ITEMS
IMMEDIATELY
AFTER CONTACT WITH
RAW MEAT

Favorite Filets

* * *

4 servings

Restaurants call this tournedos of beef or filet mignon. Actually, it doesn't matter what you call it, 'cause your gang will call it their favorite.

- ¹/₄ teaspoon salt
- ¹/₄ teaspoon black pepper
- 4 beef filet mignon steaks (6 to 8 ounces each), 1¹/₄ inches thick
- 4 strips bacon

Sprinkle the salt and pepper evenly over the steaks. In a large skillet, lightly cook the bacon over medium-high heat, but do not let it get crisp. Push the bacon to one side and leave the bacon and drippings in the skillet. In the same skillet, sauté the steaks over medium-high heat for 4 to 5 minutes per side for medium-rare, or until desired doneness. When the bacon is crisp and browned, place a slice over each steak. Remove the steaks from the pan and drain on paper towels before serving.

NOTE: A dollop of Shortcut Béarnaise Sauce (page 14) will complete your dish with all the tastes you'd get at a four-star restaurant.

Hot Striped Steak

* * *

4 servings

This steak gets its name from how it looks after being grilled on hot barbecue grill racks. And nowadays you don't even have to wait for the weather to cooperate, since you can grill indoors with a stovetop grill or a smokeless electric grill. Enjoy!

- 1/2 cup bottled steak sauce
- 1/2 teaspoon garlic powder
- 1 tablespoon hot pepper sauce
- 2 boneless beef top sirloin steaks (1 pound each)

Preheat the grill to medium-high heat. In a large bowl, combine the steak sauce, garlic powder, and hot pepper sauce; mix well. Add the steaks and turn to coat evenly with the sauce. Let sit for 5 minutes. Grill the steaks for 10 to 12 minutes, or until desired doneness, turning them over halfway through the grilling.

NOTE: Sure, this can be broiled instead of grilled. Just preheat the broiler and broil the steak to desired doneness.

Pork 'n' Cider Crisp

* * *

4 servings

How does this sound? Pork chops and fresh apples cooked in cider. Sound too good to be true? Well, it *is* true now. (It's like having apple crisp for dinner. Mmm!)

¹/₄ cup all-purpose flour
4 pork shoulder chops (1¹/₂ to 2 pounds total), about 1 inch thick
¹/₄ cup (¹/₂ stick) butter
1 small onion, chopped
¹/₄ teaspoon salt
2 large apples, peeled, cored, and chopped
1 tablespoon cornstarch
1 teaspoon ground cinnamon
1 cup apple juice
1 tablespoon light brown sugar

USE OR FREEZE LEFTOVERS AS SOON AS POSSIBLE

Place the flour in a shallow dish and completely coat the pork chops with the flour. In a large skillet, melt the butter over medium-high heat; add the pork chops and cook, uncovered, for about 5 minutes on each side, until browned. Add the onion, salt, and apples; cover and cook for 10 more minutes, turning the chops once. In a small bowl, combine the remaining ingredients, mix well, and add to the skillet. Reduce the heat to medium and continue cooking for 3 to 4 minutes, or until the sauce begins to thicken. Serve the chops topped with the sauce.

Cheesy Baked Pork Chops

* * *

4 servings

Crispy, cheesy coating on the outside...juicy pork chop on the inside.

1 cup finely crushed cheese crackers

$1/4$ cup sesame seeds

1 tablespoon chopped fresh parsley

$1/2$ teaspoon salt

$1/4$ teaspoon black pepper

$1/4$ teaspoon cayenne pepper

2 eggs

4 pork loin chops ($1^{1}/_4$ to $1^{1}/_2$ pounds total), 1 inch thick

Nonstick vegetable spray

Preheat the oven to 400°F. In a shallow bowl, combine the cracker crumbs, sesame seeds, parsley, salt, and peppers; mix well. Beat the eggs in another shallow bowl. Dip each pork chop into the eggs, then the crumb mixture, coating well. Place the chops in a 9" × 13" baking dish that has been coated with nonstick vegetable spray. Spray both sides of the chops with nonstick vegetable spray. Bake for 40 to 45 minutes, or until medium or to desired doneness beyond that, turning halfway through the cooking.

FOR A LEANER FINISHED DISH, TRIM EXCESS FAT BEFORE COOKING

Almost-Stuffed Pork Chops

* * *

4 servings

I love stuffed pork chops, but they always seemed to be so much work. Well, I've come up with a shortcut and the taste is still as good as I remember. Oh, yes, with a lot less work.

4 pork loin chops (1¼ to 1½ pounds total), 1 inch thick
Juice of 1 lime (about 2 tablespoons)
1⅓ cups coarsely crumbled cracker crumbs (about 4 ounces crackers)
6 ounces fresh mushrooms, finely chopped (about 1 cup)
3 scallions, chopped
1 tablespoon Dijon-style mustard
1 tablespoon dried parsley flakes

Preheat the oven to 350°F. Brush both sides of the pork chops with the lime juice and lay them in a 9" × 13" baking dish that has been coated with nonstick vegetable spray. In a medium-sized bowl, combine the remaining ingredients. Mix until well blended and spoon evenly over the top of the chops. Bake for 40 to 45 minutes, or until cooked through.

NOTE: These can be prepared, covered, and refrigerated overnight before baking. That way, you can put a fancy dinner on the table without having to do any last-minute preparation. (I like that!) Oh, and for a little extra oomph, I sometimes add ½ teaspoon dried ground coriander.

South Pacific Pork Chops

* * *

4 to 6 servings

Hawaii is famous for its sweet, delicious pineapples. I thought it would be fun to add them to pork chops for a real South Pacific flavor.

1 can (20 ounces) pineapple chunks, drained and liquid reserved
1¼ cups ketchup
1 tablespoon dark or light brown sugar
1 tablespoon cider vinegar
3 carrots, sliced into ¼-inch rounds
½ of a medium-sized green bell pepper, cut into chunks
2 tablespoons vegetable oil
4 to 6 pork loin chops (1½ to 2 pounds total), 1 inch thick

Preheat the oven to 350°F. In a large saucepan, heat the reserved pineapple juice, ketchup, brown sugar, and vinegar over medium heat for 5 minutes, until hot. Stir in the pineapple chunks, carrots, and pepper; remove from the heat. In a large skillet, heat the oil over medium-high heat and brown the chops for 3 to 4 minutes per side, or until browned on both sides. Place the chops in a shallow baking dish that has been coated with nonstick vegetable spray and spoon the pineapple mixture over the top. Cover with aluminum foil and bake for 1 hour, or until the chops are cooked through and the vegetables are tender.

NOTE: Be sure to have some hot cooked rice to go along with this.

Silky-Smooth Pepper Chops

* * *

4 servings

I call these silky-smooth 'cause the sauce is so creamy and delicious—a perfect match for pork chops.

1 tablespoon olive oil
2 garlic cloves, minced
4 pork rib chops (1½ to 2 pounds total), about 1 inch thick
½ cup sour cream
½ cup heavy cream
¼ teaspoon dried thyme
½ teaspoon salt
2 teaspoons black pepper

In a large skillet, heat the oil over medium heat and sauté the garlic for 1 to 2 minutes, or until golden. Add the pork chops and cook for 10 to 12 minutes, turning once. Remove the chops from the skillet and drain the excess liquid from the skillet. Reduce the heat to low and add the remaining ingredients to the skillet; mix well. Heat the mixture for 2 to 3 minutes, until heated through. Return the chops to the skillet and coat with the sauce. Continue cooking for 6 to 8 more minutes, until medium, or to desired doneness beyond that. Spoon sauce over the cooked chops.

NOTE: For a fuller black pepper flavor, use fresh-cracked black peppercorns. Simply grind the pepper in a pepper mill or, if you don't have one, place 2 teaspoons whole peppercorns in a resealable plastic storage bag. Seal the bag and use a mallet or rolling pin to crack the peppercorns on a durable surface.

Cherry Cola Country Pork Ribs

* * *

4 to 5 servings

Between my grandkids loving cherry cola and memories of loving my first cherry cola in high school, I thought there might be a good way to bring that taste to dinner. . . and there is!

  2 tablespoons vegetable oil
  4 to 5 pounds country-style pork ribs
  1 can (12 ounces) carbonated cherry cola or cola beverage
  1 bottle (12 ounces) chili sauce
  2 tablespoons Worcestershire sauce
  2 tablespoons hot pepper sauce
  1 jar (10 ounces) maraschino cherries in their own juice

In a soup pot, heat the oil over medium-high heat and brown the ribs on all sides, 8 to 10 minutes. Meanwhile, in a large bowl, combine the remaining ingredients; mix well. Reduce the heat to medium and drain off the excess liquid. Pour the cola mixture over the ribs and cook for 1½ hours, or until the ribs are cooked through and tender, turning occasionally.

NOTE: I like to use country-style ribs 'cause they're meatier, but spareribs will taste good, too.

Dill Pork Chop Bake

* * *

4 servings

So crunchy and fresh-tasting...

    1 cup seasoned bread crumbs
    2 teaspoons dried dill
    1/4 teaspoon onion powder
    1/2 teaspoon salt
    1/4 teaspoon black pepper
    2 eggs, beaten
    4 pork loin chops (1 1/4 to 1 1/2 pounds total), 1 inch thick
    Nonstick vegetable spray

Preheat the oven to 400°F. In a shallow bowl, combine the bread crumbs, dill, onion powder, salt, and pepper; mix well. Place the beaten eggs in another shallow bowl. Dip each pork chop into the eggs, then the crumb mixture, coating well. Place the chops in a 9" × 13" baking dish that has been coated with nonstick vegetable spray. Spray both sides of the chops with nonstick vegetable spray. Bake for 40 to 45 minutes, until medium, or to desired doneness beyond that, turning halfway through the cooking.

THOROUGHLY
WASH HANDS
OR ANY ITEMS
IMMEDIATELY
AFTER CONTACT WITH
RAW MEAT

Lemon-Pepper Lamb Chops

* * *

6 servings

Lamb shoulder chops are meatier than rib chops and less expensive, too. In this case, less is more.

2 tablespoons butter
6 lamb shoulder chops (2¼ to 2½ pounds total), about 1 inch thick
Juice of 1 lemon (2 to 3 tablespoons)
1 teaspoon salt
1½ teaspoons black pepper

In a large skillet, melt the butter over medium heat and cook the lamb chops for 3 minutes per side, until lightly browned. Add the lemon juice and sprinkle with the salt and pepper. Continue cooking, turning occasionally, for 12 to 14 minutes, or until the chops are done to medium or to desired doneness beyond that.

FOR A LEANER FINISHED DISH,
TRIM EXCESS FAT BEFORE COOKING

Minty Lamb Chops

* * *

4 servings

Don't ask me how lamb chops and mint jelly ever got together, but for years it's been a really popular combo. And now, with the addition of a few spices, I think we've got another winner!

   1/2 teaspoon salt
   1/2 teaspoon onion powder
   1/2 teaspoon ground sage
   4 lamb shoulder chops (2 pounds total), 3/4 inch thick
   1/4 cup mint jelly

Preheat the oven to 400°F. In a small bowl, combine the salt, onion powder, and sage; mix well. Place the lamb chops about 1 inch apart in a large baking dish that has been coated with nonstick vegetable spray. Sprinkle the mixture over both sides of the lamb chops. Bake for 25 to 30 minutes, or until desired doneness. Drain the excess liquid and top each chop with a dollop of mint jelly. Return to the oven for 2 to 3 minutes, or until the jelly begins to melt. Serve with the pan drippings.

> FOR A LEANER FINISHED DISH,
> TRIM EXCESS FAT BEFORE COOKING

Tarragon Veal Chops

* * *

4 servings

I fell in love with the taste of tarragon the first time I had béarnaise sauce with filet mignon. Now I'm using that same rich taste as the perfect accent for tender veal chops.

    2 teaspoons ground dried tarragon
    1 teaspoon salt
    ¼ teaspoon black pepper
    4 veal rib chops (2 pounds total), 1 inch thick
    ½ cup ready-to-use chicken broth

In a small bowl, combine the tarragon, salt, and pepper; mix well. Rub evenly over both sides of the veal chops. Coat a large skillet with non-stick vegetable spray. Brown the veal chops over medium heat for 3 to 4 minutes per side, or until well browned. Add the chicken broth to the skillet, increase the heat to high, and stir to mix with the pan juices. Cook for 3 to 4 minutes, or until the sauce is slightly thickened. Serve the veal chops topped with the sauce.

NOTE: Simple baked white potatoes or yams are the perfect go-along for these.

So-Stuffed Veal Chops

* * *

4 servings

Veal rib chops are perfect for stuffing 'cause they're so plump and meaty. And when they're stuffed with cheese, it's like a double bonus.

4 veal rib chops (2 to 2¼ pounds total), 1 inch thick
4 thin slices (2 ounces) Havarti cheese
1 teaspoon dried basil
¼ teaspoon garlic powder
¼ teaspoon salt
¼ teaspoon black pepper
2 tablespoons butter
½ cup dry white wine

Using a sharp knife, make a pocket in each veal chop by cutting in from the curved outer edge of the chop. (This isn't hard to do, but it's even easier to have your butcher do it.) Place a slice of cheese in each pocket and seal with toothpicks. In a small bowl, combine the basil, garlic powder, salt, and pepper; rub into both sides of the chops. In a large skillet, melt the butter over medium heat and brown the chops for 2 to 3 minutes per side. Add the wine, cover, and reduce the heat to low. Simmer for 15 to 20 minutes, or until the chops are cooked through. Serve with the sauce from the pan spooned over the chops.

NOTE: Havarti is a super cheese 'cause it's so mild, but if you'd like, you can try a sharp Cheddar, Swiss, or even an aged blue cheese instead.

Pineapple Spareribs

* * *

4 to 5 servings

Have you ever had spareribs that were so tough that you ended up with all sauce and no meat? Well, that won't happen with these! Nope—instead, you'll get tender meat and tasty caramelized coating in every bite.

> 3 to 4 pounds pork spareribs, cut into individual ribs
> 1/2 cup cider vinegar
> 1 1/2 cups water
> 3/4 cup chili sauce
> 3/4 cup firmly packed dark or light brown sugar
> 1 1/2 teaspoons soy sauce
> 1/4 teaspoon salt
> 2 tablespoons cornstarch
> 1 can (15 to 20 ounces) pineapple chunks, 1/4 cup juice reserved

USE OR FREEZE LEFTOVERS AS SOON AS POSSIBLE

Preheat the oven to 350°F. Place the ribs in a large roasting pan that has been coated with nonstick vegetable spray. Pour the cider vinegar and water over the ribs and cover tightly with aluminum foil. Bake for 1 hour, then drain off the excess liquid. In a medium-sized bowl, combine the remaining ingredients; mix well. Pour over the spareribs and bake, uncovered, for 45 more minutes, or until the glaze begins to caramelize, basting occasionally.

T.L.C. Barbecued Ribs

* * *

3 to 4 servings

Fast food restaurants serve 'em, barbecue shacks serve 'em, but the best taste is when you make 'em at home. It must be all the T.L.C. (Tender Loving Care) we add in our own kitchens.

3 to 3½ pounds beef back ribs
1 cup ketchup
1 small onion, finely chopped
¼ cup firmly packed light brown sugar
2 tablespoons white vinegar
2 tablespoons Worcestershire sauce
2 tablespoons prepared yellow mustard

Preheat the oven to 425°F. Place the ribs meat side up in a large roasting pan. Roast for 1 hour. In a medium-sized bowl, combine the remaining ingredients; mix well and set aside. Reduce the temperature to 350°F. and bake for 35 to 45 more minutes, basting every 15 minutes with the sauce. Carefully cut into individual ribs and serve with the remaining sauce.

Chinese Spareribs

* * *

4 to 6 servings

Stop right here! For years I've been trying to make really good Chinese-style spareribs. I could never quite get the right flavor and sauce consistency—until now! Yup, I've finally created a real winner.

8 garlic cloves, minced
2 teaspoons salt
½ cup ketchup
½ cup honey
½ cup soy sauce
2 cans (10¼ ounces each) condensed beef broth
3 to 4 pounds pork spareribs, cut into individual ribs

ALWAYS DISCARD USED MARINADE

In a 9" × 13" glass baking dish, combine the garlic and salt; mix well. Add the remaining ingredients except the spareribs and blend until well mixed. Add the ribs, turning to coat well with the marinade. Cover and refrigerate for at least 4 hours, or overnight, turning occasionally. Preheat the oven to 450°F. Line a large roasting pan with aluminum foil and add ½ inch of water to the pan. Coat a roasting rack with nonstick vegetable spray and place it inside the pan. Place the spareribs crosswise on the rack, reserving the marinade for basting. Roast for 10 minutes, then reduce the heat to 350°F. and roast the ribs for 1 hour and 20 minutes, or until the ribs are tender and the glaze is crispy, basting occasionally with the reserved marinade.

NOTE: Placing the ribs in a hot oven for the first 10 minutes gives them a nice crispy coating. If you're into spicy Chinese flavor, serve these with hot mustard.

Caesar's Special Country Ribs

* * *

4 to 5 servings

These ribs are extra-special 'cause country-style ribs are meatier than traditional spareribs. That means that there's more to sink your teeth into. And boy, you're gonna want to dig right in when you get a taste of these!

    2½ to 3 pounds country-style pork ribs
    1 envelope (1.2 ounces) dry Caesar salad dressing mix
    ½ cup olive oil
    Juice of 1 lemon (2 to 3 tablespoons), divided
    1 heaping tablespoon grated Parmesan cheese

Place the ribs in a 9" × 13" glass baking dish. In a small bowl, combine the dressing mix, oil, and half of the lemon juice; mix well and pour over the ribs. Cover and refrigerate for at least 4 hours, or overnight, turning once. Preheat the oven to 350°F. Place the ribs in a roasting pan that has been coated with nonstick vegetable spray and pour the marinade over the ribs; roast for 60 minutes. Remove from the oven and sprinkle the Parmesan cheese and the remaining lemon juice over the top. Return to the oven and roast for 10 to 15 more minutes, or until the cheese is golden.

Stews and One-Pots

My earliest food memories are of my mom's stews and one-pot dishes. As I said before, my dad was a butcher who brought home different cuts of meat every day. Mom never knew what to expect, and boy, did she always turn that meat into interesting dishes. Those one-pots were comforting then, and they still are now. And now that I'm making them for myself and my family, know what I like best about them? I'll tell you. They:

- Are easy to make
- Take up just one burner on the stovetop
- Have rich, long-cooked flavor
- Are a great way to use leftover veggies, potatoes, rice, and pasta
- Give you a few meals with just one cooking
- Are a super way to extend your meal when unexpected company drops by. (You just have to add a bit more liquid while heating to stretch it, and no one will ever know!)
- Make cleanup a breeze since there's just one pot
- Are perfect year-round dishes (not just for wintertime!)

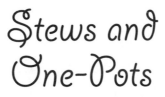

Stews and One-Pots

Stick-to-Your-Ribs Pasta Stew

* * *

6 to 8 servings

Beef, vegetables, and pasta all in one...now that's the perfect answer for a winter night's meal.

  5 cups water
  2 pounds beef top or bottom round, cut into 1-inch cubes
  1 large onion, chopped
  4 medium-sized carrots, cut into ½-inch chunks
  1½ cups ketchup
  1 jar (8 ounces) medium picante sauce
  ¼ cup Worcestershire sauce
  2 tablespoons light or dark brown sugar
  1 tablespoon salt
  1 tablespoon paprika
  8 ounces uncooked rotini pasta

In a soup pot, combine all the ingredients except the pasta. Bring to a boil, then reduce the heat to medium-low and simmer for 1 hour, stirring occasionally. Add the pasta and cook for 20 to 25 more minutes, or until the pasta is tender.

NOTE: You know how I always say there are no rules? That's certainly true here, so go ahead and use any small hearty pasta you prefer—elbows, small shells...whatever!

> FOR A LEANER FINISHED DISH,
> TRIM EXCESS FAT BEFORE COOKING

Winter Beef Stew

* * *

6 servings

When I lived in Upstate New York, I made this only on cold, wintery days. Boy, was I missing the boat! You see, now that I live in Florida, I make it no matter what the weather because I don't want to miss out on these comforting tastes that really are great anytime!

2 tablespoons all-purpose flour
2 pounds beef stew meat
3 tablespoons vegetable oil
1 teaspoon salt (optional)
$^1/_2$ teaspoon black pepper
3 cups water
2 envelopes (one 2-ounce box) onion soup mix
3 large onions, quartered
8 carrots, cut into 1-inch chunks
6 medium-sized potatoes, peeled and quartered

Place the flour in a shallow dish and coat the beef completely. In a soup pot, heat the oil over medium-high heat and brown the beef on all sides. Add the salt, pepper, water, and soup mix; bring to a boil. Reduce the heat to low, cover, and simmer for 1$^1/_2$ hours, or until the meat is almost tender. Add the onions, carrots, and potatoes and simmer for 45 minutes, or until the meat and vegetables are tender, stirring occasionally.

Heavenly Lamb Stew

* * *

4 servings

You're probably thinking, "What a combination of ingredients!" But when simmered together, they're simply heavenly!

2 tablespoons vegetable oil
1¹/₂ to 2 pounds lamb stew meat or boneless leg of lamb, cut into
   ¹/₂-inch chunks
1¹/₂ teaspoons salt
¹/₄ teaspoon black pepper
1 small onion, chopped
2 garlic cloves, minced
1 teaspoon ground cumin
1 can (17 ounces) apricot halves in heavy syrup, juice reserved

In a soup pot, heat the oil over medium-high heat and add the lamb, salt, and pepper. Cook for 7 to 10 minutes, or until the lamb is browned, stirring occasionally. Stir in the remaining ingredients. Reduce the heat to low, cover, and simmer for 40 to 45 minutes, or until the lamb is fork-tender.

NOTE: I like to serve this over hot cooked rice, noodles, or potatoes so none of the heavenly sauce gets lost!

STORE MEAT COVERED IN THE REFRIGERATOR BETWEEN 35°F. AND 40°F.

Pork Goulash

* * *

4 to 6 servings

A lot of people think one-pots all taste the same. Not true! Especially with this recipe. Its blend of spices, pork, and cream sure tastes special to me.

2 tablespoons butter
2 to 2½ pounds boneless pork loin, cut into 1-inch cubes
2 medium-sized onions, chopped
1 garlic clove, minced
2 tablespoons paprika
1 teaspoon dried dill
1 teaspoon salt
½ teaspoon black pepper
1 can (10½ ounces) condensed beef broth, divided
2 tablespoons cornstarch
½ cup heavy cream

USE OR FREEZE LEFTOVERS AS SOON AS POSSIBLE

In a large skillet, melt the butter over medium-high heat and add the pork, onions, and garlic. Sauté for 5 minutes, or until the pork is no longer pink on the outside. Stir in the paprika, dill, salt, pepper, and all but 2 tablespoons of the beef broth. Reduce the heat to low, cover, and simmer for 20 minutes. In a small bowl, whisk together the remaining beef broth and the cornstarch; pour into the skillet and stir until the sauce has thickened. Slowly add the cream and stir until warmed through.

NOTE: Don't overcook this once you add the cream, or the sauce will separate. And then there won't be any sauce left for spooning over some hot cooked egg noodles.

Dinner Sundaes

* * *

6 servings

All kids are picky eaters sometimes. Well, you can be sure they'll eat *this* time because this dish is so much fun! (And boy, does that make us happy too, 'cause it's all here—the meat, potatoes, *and vegetables!*)

     2 tablespoons vegetable oil
     1 to 1½ pounds beef flank steak, cut into ½-inch cubes
     1 jar (12 ounces) brown gravy
     1 package (10 ounces) frozen mixed vegetables, thawed and drained
     6 servings warm instant mashed potatoes
     6 cherry tomatoes

In a large skillet, heat the oil over medium heat. Add the beef and sauté for 5 to 6 minutes, or until browned. Reduce the heat to low and stir in the gravy and vegetables; simmer over low heat for 6 to 7 minutes, or until heated through. Spoon the meat mixture evenly into 6 soup bowls or sundae glasses and top with heaping dollops of potatoes. Top each sundae with a cherry tomato.

NOTE: If your kids would rather have stuffing or rice in place of the potatoes, those will work, too. Let them choose their favorite sundae flavors!

Veal Fricassee

* * *

4 to 6 servings

My mom used to make fricassee with mini-meatballs and chicken wings, but this version uses veal stew meat. It sure is a nice change!

2 to 2½ pounds veal stew meat
1 large onion, chopped
⅔ cup dry white wine
6 medium-sized carrots, cut into ½-inch chunks
2 beef bouillon cubes
2 bay leaves
¼ teaspoon dried thyme
¾ teaspoon salt
½ teaspoon black pepper
½ cup milk
¼ cup all-purpose flour
2 teaspoons browning and seasoning sauce
4 ounces fresh mushrooms, sliced (about 2 cups)

THOROUGHLY WASH HANDS OR ANY ITEMS IMMEDIATELY AFTER CONTACT WITH RAW MEAT

Preheat the oven to 325°F. In a 2-quart covered casserole dish, combine the veal, onion, wine, carrots, bouillon cubes, bay leaves, thyme, salt, and pepper; mix well. Cover and bake for 2 hours. In a small bowl, whisk together the milk, flour, and browning sauce until no lumps remain. Slowly pour the milk mixture into the casserole dish, stirring constantly until thickened. Stir in the mushrooms and bake, uncovered, for 20 to 30 more minutes, or until the mushrooms are tender. **Be sure to remove the bay leaves before serving.**

Chunky Beef Chili

* * *

8 to 10 servings

Hurray! It's all in one pot! That means that in minutes you're ready to let your stovetop do all the work (so you can get all the raves).

> 2¹/₂ to 3 pounds beef top or bottom round, cut into 1-inch cubes
> 1 teaspoon minced garlic
> 2 medium-sized green bell peppers, cut into ¹/₂-inch cubes
> 1 medium-sized onion, cut into ¹/₂-inch cubes
> 3 tablespoons chili powder
> ¹/₂ teaspoon ground cumin
> 1 can (28 ounces) crushed tomatoes
> 2 tablespoons sugar
> 2 teaspoons salt
> ¹/₂ teaspoon cayenne pepper

In a soup pot, brown the beef and garlic over medium-high heat for 12 to 14 minutes, or until no pink remains in the meat, stirring occasionally. Stir in the remaining ingredients; mix well. Bring to a boil, then reduce the heat to medium-low and simmer for 2¹/₂ to 3 hours, until thickened.

NOTE: You might want to try this chili and the one on the next page, then decide on your family favorite.

> FOR A LEANER FINISHED DISH,
> TRIM EXCESS FAT BEFORE COOKING

Fire Station Chili

* * *

8 to 10 servings

We've all heard that fire departments are known for their chili cookin', so I had to share one of their recipes. Don't be alarmed—it's simple!

2 tablespoons vegetable oil
1 large onion, chopped
3 garlic cloves, minced
2 pounds ground beef
1 can (28 ounces) crushed tomatoes
$1/3$ cup chili powder
1 teaspoon salt
1 teaspoon ground cumin
1 teaspoon black pepper
2 cans (16 ounces each) red kidney beans, drained

In a large pot, heat the oil over medium-high heat and sauté the onion and garlic for 5 minutes, or until tender. Add the ground beef and brown for 8 to 10 minutes, or until no pink remains; drain off the excess liquid. Add the remaining ingredients; mix well. Reduce the heat to low; cover and simmer for 30 minutes, stirring occasionally.

NOTE: If you want to give this a spicy kick, add 1 tablespoon hot pepper sauce along with the tomatoes.

Dunkin' Lamb One-Pot

* * *

4 to 6 servings

Maybe I should have added a hearty bread to this ingredient list, 'cause that's what makes eating this lamb so good—all the dunkin'.

    2 tablespoons olive oil
    2 to 3 garlic cloves, minced
    1 large onion, coarsely chopped
    1 to 1¼ pounds lamb stew meat or boneless leg of lamb, cut into
        1-inch chunks
    1 cup chopped fresh parsley
    2 cans (28 ounces each) whole tomatoes, drained and coarsely
        chopped
    1 can (16 ounces) garbanzo beans (chick peas), drained
    1 cup water
    1 teaspoon ground cumin
    1 teaspoon salt
    ¼ teaspoon cayenne pepper

> FOR A LEANER FINISHED DISH,
> TRIM EXCESS FAT BEFORE COOKING

In a soup pot, heat the oil over medium-high heat. Add the garlic and sauté for 1 minute, or until lightly browned. Add the onion and lamb and cook for 8 to 9 minutes, or until the onion is tender and the lamb is no longer pink. Add the remaining ingredients and bring to a boil. Reduce the heat to low, cover, and simmer for 50 to 60 minutes, or until the lamb is fork-tender.

NOTE: For a special occasion, you might want to replace ½ cup of the water with ½ cup dry white wine. Add a few croutons and you've got another great way to "dunk" without dunkin'.

Simmered Curried Lamb

* * *

6 to 8 servings

All it takes is one pan and a few ingredients to turn boneless lamb into an international favorite. I bet this makes lamb a regular main course at your house.

- ½ cup (1 stick) butter
- 2½ to 3 pounds boneless leg of lamb or lamb stew meat, cut into 1-inch cubes
- 2 medium-sized onions, chopped
- 3 tablespoons all-purpose flour
- 1 cup ready-to-use beef broth
- 2 apples, cored, peeled, and coarsely chopped
- 1 cup raisins
- 1 tablespoon curry powder
- 1 teaspoon salt
- ¼ teaspoon black pepper

In a large skillet, melt the butter over medium-high heat. Sauté the lamb chunks and onions for 12 to 15 minutes, or until no pink remains in the lamb. Stir in the flour, then the broth. Add the remaining ingredients; mix well. Reduce the heat to low, cover, and simmer for 1 hour, or until the meat is fork-tender.

NOTE: Would you guess that Granny Smith apples are one of the best types for this recipe? That's what the viewer who shared this recipe told me...and she's right!

All-in-One Hearty Ribs and Cabbage

* * *

4 to 6 servings

Mmm... meaty short ribs simmered in a flavorful tomato and cabbage soup. What could be better? It's all in one pot! Yippee!

    5 to 6 pounds beef short ribs
    2 cans (28 ounces each) crushed tomatoes
    1 can (12 ounces) tomato paste
    Juice of 1 lemon (2 to 3 tablespoons)
    3 beef bouillon cubes
    8 cups water
    1 cup granulated sugar
    ½ cup firmly packed light or dark brown sugar
    ½ of a medium-sized cabbage, chopped (4 cups)
    1 teaspoon salt

In a soup pot, brown the ribs over medium-high heat, turning to brown all sides. Reduce the heat to low and stir in the remaining ingredients. Simmer for 2½ to 3 hours, or until the meat is tender, stirring frequently.

NOTE: I like to serve the short ribs with some prepared white horseradish on the side.

USE OR FREEZE LEFTOVERS AS SOON AS POSSIBLE

From the
"Ground" Up

Meat sauce, tacos, lasagna, Sloppy Joes... the list of ground meat dishes we love goes on and on. It's easy to cook with ground meats, and there are limitless flavors we can team them with to change and enhance our dishes every time. But before you start making the mouthwatering recipes here, please read the safety tips that follow. We can all eat more safely if we prepare and cook smart:

- Raw ground meats should be rich in color. Ground beef should be bright red, and ground veal, lamb, and pork should be light pink. Ground meat that has been frozen or vacuum-packed tends to be deeper in color than fresh ground meat and it will brighten in color when opened and exposed to air.
- At home, all ground meat should be stored at 35°F. to 40°F. (see page xxvi for information on refrigerator thermometers). The refrigerator meat storage drawer or the lowest refrigerator shelf is the best, because those tend to be the coldest.

- Ground meats should be stored in the refrigerator for no more than 2 days. They should be either used or frozen by that point. Freeze ground meats in heavy-duty aluminum foil or freezer paper for up to 4 months at 0°F. or lower. **Thaw ground meats only when intending to use them right away. It is recommended that you defrost ground meats only in the refrigerator, on a defrosting tray, or in the microwave according to the manufacturer's instructions.**
- Today our butchers give us lots of ground-meat blend choices. If a label is marked "extra lean," that probably means that it's a 90 to 10 meat to fat ratio (90 percent meat and 10 percent fat). If you want to know what you're buying, simply read the labels or ask your butcher.
- Be sure to form your burger patties to a uniform thickness so that they'll cook evenly throughout.
- **According to the U.S. Department of Agriculture, it is no longer acceptable to eat ground meat cooked to any doneness but well-done. Ground meats must be cooked until absolutely no pink remains and the juices run clear. This should eliminate your chances of coming in contact with any harmful bacteria.**

- Don't let dark sauces like teriyaki and Worcestershire fool you—they usually darken the color of meat and it may make you think that the meat is done before it actually is. So, when using these and other sauces, be sure to check the color of the inside of the meat and the juices for doneness.
- For flavor and texture variation, why not try mixing your ground meats? One time use ground veal mixed with ground beef, the next try ground lamb with ground pork, and so on. It'll give you that many more ways to enjoy the versatility of ground meats.

From the "Ground" Up

Shortcut Bacon Cheeseburgers

* * *

4 burgers

This sure is an all-time favorite at just about any burger joint. But now you can make this at home without having to fry bacon first—because I use a shortcut that tastes just as good.

1 to 1¼ pounds ground beef
¼ cup bacon bits
½ cup (2 ounces) shredded Cheddar cheese
½ teaspoon salt
¼ teaspoon black pepper
¼ cup dry bread crumbs
¼ cup water
4 hamburger buns, split

In a large bowl, combine all of the ingredients except the buns. Divide the mixture into 4 equal amounts and make 4 patties. Heat a large nonstick skillet over medium heat and panfry the patties for 6 to 8 minutes, or until the juices run clear, turning occasionally. Serve the burgers on the buns.

NOTE: For a variation, why not top these with hickory-smoked barbecue sauce? It sure tastes great on them.

ALWAYS COOK GROUND MEAT UNTIL WELL-DONE, NO PINK REMAINS AND THE JUICES RUN CLEAR

Piled-High Cheeseburgers

* * *

4 burgers

After you finish topping these burgers, you're going to have to bring out the forks and knives to eat them!

- 1 to 1¼ pounds ground beef
- ½ teaspoon Worcestershire sauce
- ½ teaspoon salt
- ¼ teaspoon black pepper
- 1 can (2.8 ounces) French-fried onions
- 4 slices (4 ounces total) Monterey Jack cheese
- 4 hamburger buns, split

In a large bowl, combine the beef, Worcestershire sauce, salt, and pepper; mix well. Divide the mixture into 4 equal amounts and make 4 patties. Heat a medium-sized nonstick skillet over medium heat and panfry the patties for 6 to 8 minutes, or until the juices run clear, turning occasionally. Leave the burgers in the skillet and remove it from the heat. Top the burgers evenly with the French-fried onions and the cheese. Cover the skillet and cook over low heat for 2 to 3 more minutes, or until the cheese has melted. Place the burgers on the buns and serve.

NOTE: To make these mile-high cheeseburgers, pile them with all your favorites: lettuce, tomatoes, pickles, jalapeño peppers, and more!

Pretzel Burgers

* * *

4 burgers

Pretzels are more popular than ever. We always knew how great they tasted, but now we like them even more because they're also relatively low in fat. So when we mix them with lean ground beef we can make burgers that are lower in fat but higher in flavor!

    1 to 1¼ pounds ground beef
    ½ cup crushed pretzels and 4 whole twist pretzels
    1 egg
    1 teaspoon onion powder
    1 teaspoon black pepper

Preheat the oven to 375°F. In a medium-sized bowl, combine all the ingredients except the whole pretzels; mix well. Divide the mixture into 4 equal amounts and make 4 patties. Place the patties on a cookie sheet that has been coated with nonstick vegetable spray and press a pretzel gently onto the top of each. Bake for 8 to 10 minutes, or until the juices run clear.

NOTE: Depending on how salty your pretzels are, you may want to add some salt to the ground beef mixture.

Lie down right there!

Pepper Parmesan Burgers

* * *

4 burgers

You've enjoyed this taste in dressing, now try it in burgers. It's a simple way to spice up your burgers for a completely new and original flavor.

1 to 1¼ pounds ground beef
½ teaspoon salt
2 teaspoons black pepper
½ cup grated Parmesan cheese
¼ cup dry bread crumbs
¼ cup water
4 hamburger buns, split

In a large bowl, combine all of the ingredients except the buns; mix well. Divide the mixture into 4 equal amounts and make 4 patties. Heat a large nonstick skillet over medium heat and panfry the patties for 7 to 9 minutes, or until the juices run clear, turning occasionally. Serve the burgers on the buns.

NOTE: If you want to go a step further, serve these with sliced tomatoes and lettuce, in addition to your favorite condiments.

ALWAYS
WASH HANDS
BEFORE AND AFTER
HANDLING RAW MEAT

Veal Cordon Bleu Burgers

* * *

4 burgers

It's easy to get away from the traditional "burgers on the grill." And when you start with ground veal, you know you're in for a treat!

1¼ to 1½ pounds ground veal
¼ cup seasoned bread crumbs
1 egg
¾ teaspoon salt
½ teaspoon black pepper
4 thin slices (3 ounces total) deli ham
4 slices (4 ounces total) Swiss cheese, cut in half

In a large bowl, combine the veal, bread crumbs, egg, salt, and pepper; mix well. Divide the mixture into 8 equal amounts and make 8 patties. Top each of 4 patties with a piece of ham and a piece of cheese. Fold the ham over the cheese, then top each with another veal patty. (See diagram opposite.) Use your fingers to pinch and seal the patty edges. Coat a large skillet with nonstick vegetable spray. Heat the skillet over medium heat and cook the burgers for 14 to 16 minutes, or until no pink remains, turning once. During the last 2 minutes of cooking, place a piece of cheese on top of each patty. Cover the pan until the cheese has melted.

STORE MEAT COVERED IN THE REFRIGERATOR BETWEEN 35°F. AND 40°F.

SWISS CHEESE

VEAL PATTY

HAM

SWISS

VEAL PATTY

CORDON BLEU

Meat Loaf and Potato Casserole

* * *

4 servings

Here's a great meat-and-potatoes combination that's sure to be a hit with your gang!

1 pound lean ground beef
1/3 cup saltine cracker crumbs (about 8 crackers)
1 medium-sized onion, finely chopped
1 egg, lightly beaten
1 tablespoon chili powder
3/4 teaspoon salt
4 servings warm instant mashed potatoes
1 can (11 ounces) whole-kernel corn, drained
6 scallions, thinly sliced
1/2 cup (2 ounces) shredded Cheddar cheese

Preheat the oven to 375°F. In a large bowl, combine the ground beef, cracker crumbs, onion, egg, chili powder, and salt; mix well. Press the mixture into an 8-inch square baking dish that has been coated with nonstick vegetable spray and bake for 25 to 30 minutes, or until the juices run clear. Drain off the excess liquid. Combine the potatoes, corn, and scallions. Spread over the meat loaf. Sprinkle the cheese evenly over the top. Bake for 8 to 10 more minutes, or until the cheese has melted and the top has begun to brown.

NOTE: If you want to add more spicy heat, use a little more chili powder or use a blend of shredded Mexican cheeses or Monterey Jack cheese with jalapeño peppers instead of Cheddar cheese.

French Meat Loaf

* * *

6 to 8 servings

Meat loaf has always been an American classic and now, with a twist, our classic becomes a European-tasting dinner in no time.

1½ to 2 pounds ground beef
1½ small onions, finely chopped
1 cup dry bread crumbs
1 cup (4 ounces) shredded Cheddar cheese
½ cup sweet-and-spicy French dressing
2 eggs
1 can (4 ounces) mushrooms, drained
½ teaspoon salt
½ teaspoon black pepper
½ cup ketchup

Preheat the oven to 375°F. In a large bowl, combine all of the ingredients except the ketchup; mix well. Place in a 5" × 9" loaf pan that has been coated with nonstick vegetable spray. Spread the ketchup evenly over the top. Bake for 1 to 1¼ hours, or until the juices run clear. Allow to sit for 5 minutes. Pour off the excess liquid, slice, and serve.

NOTE: Served cold on white bread, slices of this meat loaf make a tasty late-night (or anytime) sandwich snack.

ALWAYS COOK
GROUND MEAT UNTIL
WELL-DONE:
NO PINK REMAINS AND
THE JUICES RUN CLEAR

Potato-Stuffed Meat Loaf

* * *

4 to 6 servings

Meat loaf has always been a family favorite, but when it's stuffed with mashed potatoes, you get two favorites in every bite.

1½ cups instant mashed potato flakes
1 cup water
½ cup sour cream
½ teaspoon salt
2 eggs
1 to 1½ pounds ground beef
1 small onion, finely chopped
1 medium-sized green bell pepper, finely chopped
1 cup seasoned bread crumbs
¾ cup milk
2 tablespoons steak sauce

Preheat the oven to 350°F. In a medium-sized bowl, combine the potato flakes, water, sour cream, salt, and 1 egg; mix well and set aside. In another medium-sized bowl, combine the remaining ingredients; mix well. Pat half of the meat mixture into a 5" × 9" loaf pan that has been coated with nonstick vegetable spray. Press the meat down and make a ½-inch indentation down the middle length of the loaf. Fill the indentation with the potato mixture. Gently top with the remaining meat, pressing the meat down over and around the potato filling. Bake for 55 to 60 minutes, or until the juices run clear. Allow to sit for 5 minutes before slicing.

USE OR FREEZE LEFTOVERS AS SOON AS POSSIBLE

Garden Eggplant Meat Loaf

* * *

6 to 8 servings

I know, meat loaf doesn't grow in a garden—but eggplant, onions, and garlic do. Another thing I know is that this meat loaf will grow on *you* after just one taste!

1/2 of a medium-sized eggplant, peeled and cut into 1-inch cubes
1 medium-sized onion, quartered
2 garlic cloves
1/4 cup olive oil
2 pounds ground beef or veal
3 eggs
1 cup Italian-style bread crumbs
1/4 cup grated Parmesan cheese
1 tablespoon Italian seasoning
1 teaspoon black pepper

Preheat the oven to 350°F. Place the eggplant, onion, garlic, and oil in a food processor that has been fitted with a cutting blade. Pulse for 15 to 20 seconds, or until finely chopped. Place the mixture into a medium-sized skillet and cook over medium heat for 8 to 10 minutes, until well cooked. In a large bowl, combine the remaining ingredients; mix well. Add the vegetable mixture to the meat mixture; stir until well mixed. On a rimmed baking sheet that has been coated with non-stick vegetable spray, form the mixture into a 5" × 12" loaf. Bake for 1 1/4 to 1 1/2 hours, or until the juices run clear. Allow to sit for 5 minutes before slicing.

NOTE: I've made this by combining 1 pound of ground beef and 1 pound of ground veal. That gives it a little lighter taste.

Muffin Tin Meat Loaves

* * *

12 meat loaf muffins

Kids will love them 'cause they're fun to eat. You'll love them 'cause they cook up so fast. Make a double batch and keep 'em on hand for a quick snack or meal... no kidding!

1½ pounds lean ground beef
1 medium-sized zucchini, shredded
1 cup dry bread crumbs
1 egg, slightly beaten
1 teaspoon Italian seasoning
½ teaspoon salt
¼ cup ketchup

Preheat the oven to 400°F. In a large bowl, combine all the ingredients except the ketchup, mixing lightly but thoroughly. Place about ⅓ cup of the beef mixture into each of 12 ungreased medium-sized muffin cups, pressing lightly; spread the ketchup over the tops. Bake for 20 minutes, or until no pink remains and the juices run clear.

NOTE: Not only is this a quick dinner, but it's a great way for kids of all ages to enjoy all-in-one meat and veggie muffins!

ALWAYS COOK GROUND MEAT UNTIL WELL-DONE. NO PINK REMAINS AND THE JUICES RUN CLEAR

Tomorrow's Shepherd's Pie

* * *

6 to 8 servings

I always prepared this the day before I was going to serve it. You guessed it! That's how it got its name. You're going to love it, too, 'cause all you'll have to do when you get home from work is pop it in the oven. Then, presto! You'll have dinner in minutes.

1 to 1½ pounds lean ground beef
1 medium-sized onion, chopped
1 envelope (1 ounce) onion soup mix
1 can (10½ ounces) beef gravy
1 teaspoon garlic powder
½ teaspoon black pepper
1 can (7 ounces) whole-kernel corn, drained
1 can (16 ounces) sliced carrots, drained
1 package (10 ounces) frozen peas, thawed and drained
8 servings warm instant mashed potatoes
Paprika for sprinkling

STORE MEAT COVERED IN THE REFRIGERATOR BETWEEN 35°F. AND 40°F.

Preheat the oven to 350°F. In a large skillet, brown the ground beef and chopped onion. Drain off any excess liquid. Add the soup mix, gravy, garlic powder, and pepper; mix well. Add the corn, carrots, and peas; mix well. Place in a 2-quart casserole dish that has been coated with nonstick vegetable spray. Spread the mashed potatoes over the top and sprinkle with paprika. Bake for 25 minutes, or until heated through.

NOTE: If you *do* make this the day before serving, don't bake it until just before you plan to eat it. It should take 35 to 40 minutes to heat through after it's been stored in the refrigerator.

Homestyle Sloppy Joes

* * *

6 to 8 servings

I've always wondered where these came from, and to tell you the truth, I haven't found the answer yet. All I know is that they *are* messy to eat—but that's half the fun!

    2 to 2¹/₂ pounds ground beef
    1 medium-sized onion, chopped
    1 medium-sized green bell pepper, chopped
    2 cans (15 ounces each) tomato sauce
    2 tablespoons light or dark brown sugar
    ¹/₂ teaspoon garlic powder
    ¹/₂ teaspoon salt
    ¹/₄ teaspoon black pepper
    8 sandwich or hamburger buns, split

In a large skillet, brown the ground beef, onion, and green pepper over medium-high heat for 7 to 9 minutes; drain off the excess liquid. Add the remaining ingredients except the buns; mix well. Reduce the heat to low and simmer for 8 to 10 minutes, stirring occasionally. Serve over the buns.

NOTE: For some extra zing, add 1 teaspoon hot pepper sauce. Oh— don't forget the napkins!

Diner Salisbury Steak

* * *

4 servings

I was on the road a lot last year and found myself eating a lot of hamburgers. Even though I love a good burger, I can eat only so many of them. Then I switched to Salisbury steak and was happy to have a ground beef alternative to burgers. It's great at home, too, 'cause it's still inexpensive, still fast, and still full of "OOH IT'S SO GOOD!!®"

1¼ to 1½ pounds ground beef
1 small onion, finely chopped
¼ cup seasoned bread crumbs
1 egg
2 tablespoons chopped fresh parsley
1 teaspoon prepared horseradish
1 teaspoon salt
2 cups sliced fresh mushrooms (5 ounces)
1 can (10½ ounces) mushroom gravy

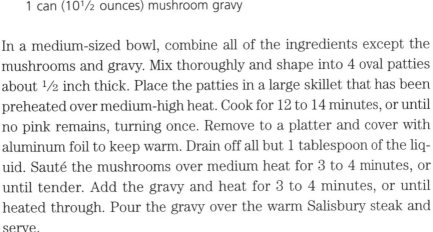

ALWAYS COOK
GROUND MEAT UNTIL
WELL-DONE,
NO PINK REMAINS AND
THE JUICES RUN CLEAR

In a medium-sized bowl, combine all of the ingredients except the mushrooms and gravy. Mix thoroughly and shape into 4 oval patties about ½ inch thick. Place the patties in a large skillet that has been preheated over medium-high heat. Cook for 12 to 14 minutes, or until no pink remains, turning once. Remove to a platter and cover with aluminum foil to keep warm. Drain off all but 1 tablespoon of the liquid. Sauté the mushrooms over medium heat for 3 to 4 minutes, or until tender. Add the gravy and heat for 3 to 4 minutes, or until heated through. Pour the gravy over the warm Salisbury steak and serve.

NOTE: I like mine a bit more peppery than most, so I usually add ¼ teaspoon of black pepper, too.

American Goulash

* * *

4 to 6 servings

"Stars and Stripes Forever"...and goulash, too! That's what you'll think once you put your fork into this American classic.

 1½ to 2 pounds ground beef
 ½ of a medium-sized green bell pepper, chopped
 1 small onion, chopped
 1 jar (28 ounces) spaghetti sauce
 1 tablespoon garlic salt
 ½ teaspoon black pepper
 8 ounces uncooked elbow macaroni
 ½ cup water
 1 cup (4 ounces) shredded mozzarella cheese

Preheat the oven to 350°F. In a large skillet, brown the ground beef, bell pepper, and onion over medium-high heat for 6 to 8 minutes, or until no pink remains in the beef, stirring frequently. Drain off the excess liquid. Add the remaining ingredients except the cheese; mix well. Place in a 2½-quart casserole dish that has been coated with nonstick vegetable spray; cover and bake for 25 minutes. Remove from the oven and top with the mozzarella cheese. Return to the oven and bake, uncovered, for 15 to 20 more minutes, or until thoroughly heated and the cheese has melted.

NOTE: This is a perfect dish to make ahead and freeze. You can even freeze it in individual portions so that way the kids can microwave a dish after school or anytime they need a quick meal.

WRAP FOOD WELL BEFORE FREEZING

Garden Spanish Rice

* * *

6 to 8 servings

I practically grew up on Spanish rice. Sometimes Mom made it with meat, and sometimes without. Today's meat version gives us a whole meal in one. And with all the chopped onion, pepper, and tomato, it sure tastes garden fresh.

1 to 1 1/2 pounds ground beef
1 medium-sized onion, coarsely chopped
1 medium-sized green bell pepper, coarsely chopped
2 cans (14 1/2 ounces each) stewed tomatoes
2 cups water
1 1/2 cups long- or whole-grain rice
1 1/2 teaspoons salt
1/4 teaspoon black pepper
1 teaspoon chili powder
1/2 teaspoon garlic powder
2 tablespoons Worcestershire sauce

In a soup pot, brown the ground beef over medium-high heat for 4 to 5 minutes, stirring frequently. Drain off the excess liquid. Add the onion and bell pepper and sauté for 4 to 5 minutes, or until the pepper is tender. Add the remaining ingredients and bring to a boil. Reduce the heat to low, cover, and simmer for 20 minutes. Remove from the heat and allow to sit, covered, for 30 to 35 minutes, or until the liquid is absorbed; serve.

Far East Beef and Rice

* * *

6 to 8 servings

This ground beef dish gives you everything you could want all in one pot. And the best thing is, it's packed with flavor.

1 to 1½ pounds ground beef
1 garlic clove, minced
1½ tablespoons vegetable oil, divided
1 medium-sized red bell pepper, cut into ½-inch strips
5 ounces fresh mushrooms, cut into ½-inch slices (about 2 cups)
4 ounces fresh pea pods, trimmed
¼ teaspoon ground ginger
3 cups cooked rice
½ cup soy sauce
2 eggs, beaten

> ALWAYS COOK GROUND MEAT UNTIL WELL-DONE, NO PINK REMAINS AND THE JUICES RUN CLEAR

In a large deep nonstick skillet or wok, brown the beef and garlic over medium heat for 8 to 10 minutes, or until no pink remains in the beef. Remove the beef to a bowl and drain off the excess liquid; set the beef aside. In the same skillet, heat 1 tablespoon oil over medium-high heat. Stir-fry the pepper, mushrooms, and pea pods for 3 to 4 minutes, just until tender. Add the beef and the remaining ingredients except the eggs. Cook for 4 to 5 minutes, or until heated through. Add the eggs and stir constantly for 2 to 3 minutes, or until the eggs are cooked through. Serve immediately.

NOTE: You can add a little extra crunch and color with 2 chopped scallions.

No-Fuss Lasagna

* * *

6 to 8 servings

No precooking noodles, no fancy ingredients. Now that's my kind of dish!

1 pound lean ground beef
1/4 teaspoon salt
1/4 teaspoon cayenne pepper
1 jar (28 ounces) spaghetti sauce
1 can (14 1/2 ounces) Italian-style diced tomatoes
1 package (10 ounces) frozen spinach, thawed and well drained

1 container (15 ounces) ricotta cheese
1/4 cup grated Parmesan cheese
1 egg, beaten
10 uncooked lasagna noodles
1 1/2 cups (6 ounces) shredded mozzarella cheese, divided

Preheat the oven to 375°F. In a large skillet, cook the ground beef over medium heat for 8 to 10 minutes, or until browned. Drain off the excess liquid. Add the salt, pepper, spaghetti sauce, and tomatoes; stir until well blended, then set aside. In a medium-sized bowl, combine the spinach, ricotta and Parmesan cheeses, and the egg; mix well. Spread 2 cups of the sauce mixture over the bottom of a 9" × 13" baking dish that has been coated with nonstick vegetable spray. Lightly press 4 noodles lengthwise over the sauce and 1 noodle across the end of the baking dish, completely covering the sauce mixture. Spread the ricotta mixture evenly over the noodles, then sprinkle with 1 cup mozzarella cheese. Top with 1 1/2 cups of the sauce mixture, then arrange the remaining noodles over the sauce, pressing lightly into the sauce. Spread the remaining sauce over the top. Bake for 45 minutes, or until the noodles are tender. Remove from the oven and sprinkle with the remaining 1/2 cup mozzarella; cover with aluminum foil. Let sit for 15 minutes, then cut and serve.

Muy Bueno Tacos

* * *

12 tacos

Did you know that *muy bueno* is Spanish for "very good"? That's exactly what these tacos are!

1 to 1½ pounds ground beef
1 large onion, chopped, divided
½ of a medium-sized green bell pepper, chopped
2 tablespoons Taco Seasoning (opposite page)
½ cup mild picante sauce
12 taco shells
1 to 2 cups shredded lettuce
1 cup (4 ounces) shredded Cheddar cheese
1 cup chopped tomato

Preheat the oven to 350°F. In a large skillet, brown the ground beef, ½ cup onions, and bell pepper over medium heat for 8 to 10 minutes, or until no pink remains in the beef. Drain off the excess liquid and stir in the Taco Seasoning and picante sauce; mix well. Reduce the heat to low and simmer for 3 to 4 minutes; remove from the heat. Place the taco shells on a cookie sheet and bake for 5 to 7 minutes, or until crisp. Remove from the oven and fill each shell ⅓ full with the meat mixture, then top with the remaining onion, the lettuce, cheese, and tomato.

NOTE: You can also top each of these with a dollop of sour cream or guacamole sauce, if you'd like. And if you're one of those people who like things a little spicy, you can use medium or hot picante sauce instead of mild!

STORE MEAT COVERED IN THE REFRIGERATOR BETWEEN 35°F. AND 40°F.

Taco Seasoning

* * *

About ½ cup

Isn't it time for you to prepare your own taco seasoning mix? Sure, you can make one just as good as store-bought—or better—at home. Make some of this and keep it on hand for whenever you get the urge to make a Tex-Mex dish. And you can adjust it to your own level of spiciness by adding more or less chili powder or even a dash of cayenne pepper!

  ¼ cup chili powder
  2 teaspoons ground cumin
  2 teaspoons salt
  4 teaspoons dried oregano
  4 teaspoons paprika

Place all of the ingredients in a small plastic container with a tight-fitting lid and shake to mix. Use as much as you like to season your favorite recipes with homemade Tex-Mex zip.

NOTE: Add to Muy Bueno Tacos (opposite page) or rub generously all over raw steaks or roasts before cooking to desired doneness.

Lamb Kebab Sandwiches

* * *

6 sandwiches

I used to shape these on skewers to make traditional kebabs, until I tried making them into sandwiches and decided I liked them this way even better! Oh... I can still call 'em kebabs, can't I?

1 large cucumber, seeds removed and finely chopped
1 container (8 ounces) plain yogurt
1¼ teaspoons salt, divided
¾ teaspoon garlic powder, divided
½ teaspoon black pepper, divided
2 to 2½ pounds ground lamb
1 small onion, finely chopped
½ cup finely chopped fresh parsley
Six 6- to 8-inch pitas

ALWAYS COOK
GROUND MEAT UNTIL
WELL-DONE
NO PINK REMAINS AND
THE JUICES RUN CLEAR

In a medium-sized bowl, combine the cucumber, yogurt, and ¼ teaspoon each of the salt, garlic powder, and pepper; mix well, cover, and chill for 1 hour. Preheat the oven to 350°F. In a medium-sized bowl, combine the remaining unused ingredients except the pitas; mix well. Roll the meat mixture into 2-inch meatballs and place on a rimmed cookie sheet. Flatten the meatballs with the palm of your hand and bake for 20 to 25 minutes, or until the lamb is no longer pink. Cut the pitas in half and open the pockets. Place 1 to 2 lamb patties inside each pita pocket and serve with the cucumber sauce.

Beefy Garlic Pizza

* * *

6 to 8 slices

Did I say garlic? You betcha! This is purely for the garlic lovers among us!

2 tablespoons vegetable oil
1 fresh garlic bulb, peeled and separated into cloves (see Note)
1 pound ground beef
3 plum tomatoes, seeded and chopped
1 teaspoon salt
1 teaspoon black pepper
One 12- to 14-inch (16-ounce) prepared pizza shell, thawed if frozen
1 package (6 ounces) sliced provolone cheese

Preheat the oven to 450°F. In a large skillet, heat the oil over medium-high heat and sauté the garlic for 4 to 5 minutes, until golden brown. Add the ground beef and cook for 8 to 10 minutes, or until completely browned, stirring frequently. Drain off the excess liquid and stir in the tomatoes, salt, and pepper. Place the pizza shell on a pan and spoon the mixture onto the pizza shell. Top with the cheese and bake for 11 to 13 minutes, or until the crust is crisp and brown. Cut and serve.

NOTE: If the garlic cloves aren't all about the same size, cut the bigger ones in half or in quarters. That way, they'll all cook evenly.

Sage Breakfast Sausage

* * *

16 patties

What a perfect way to celebrate a new day! Yup, with homemade breakfast sausage that's easy enough to make anytime! Boy, won't they be impressed when you tell them you made it from scratch!

    1 pound ground pork or veal
    ³/₄ teaspoon salt
    ³/₄ teaspoon black pepper
    2 teaspoons ground sage
    ¹/₈ teaspoon ground nutmeg
    2 tablespoons vegetable oil

In a medium-sized bowl, combine all the ingredients except the oil; mix well. Divide the mixture into 16 equal amounts and make 16 patties. Heat the oil in a large skillet over medium-high heat and panfry the patties for 6 to 8 minutes, or until no pink remains.

NOTE: This isn't just for breakfast—it's good anytime! And crumbled and browned in a skillet until no pink remains, the seasoned meat makes a great pizza topping or a hearty addition to any soup or sauce.

THOROUGHLY
WASH HANDS
OR ANY ITEMS
IMMEDIATELY
AFTER CONTACT WITH
RAW MEAT

Homemade Spicy Sausage

* * *

16 links

Did you ever imagine you'd be making sausage at home? Sure, you can do it! (It's so easy when you don't have to worry about filling a casing.)

1 pound ground pork
1 small onion, chopped
1 teaspoon dried thyme
1 teaspoon salt
1 teaspoon fennel seed, crushed
1/2 teaspoon garlic powder
1/2 teaspoon black pepper
1/4 teaspoon cayenne pepper
2 tablespoons vegetable oil

In a medium-sized bowl, combine all the ingredients except the oil; mix well. Form the mixture into 3-inch-long sausage links. In a large skillet, heat the oil over medium-high heat and cook the links, turning, for 6 to 8 minutes, or until no pink remains.

NOTE: This is *your* homemade sausage, so if you prefer ground beef or veal instead of pork, go ahead and use it. It's up to you. And if you'd rather have patties instead of links, that's okay, too. Or just brown it up without forming links; it's a great pizza topping that way (or a tomato sauce addition, too)!

Stovetop Favorites

No need to fire up the grill or light the oven with these! And they're quick-cooking and flavor-packed, too! Yup, these are recipes that are prepared right on your stovetop. Some are cooked with dry heat for quick searing, which seals in the flavorful juices. Others are mixed and matched with vegetables and other ingredients for cooking with moist heat. Both give you results that are tender and tasty every time.

I've got some new ideas here, along with some oldies that I've updated in the **Mr. Food®** style. They should take the ho-hum out of mealtime with a saucy stir-fried, sautéed, or simmered stovetop "OOH IT'S SO GOOD!!®"

Here are some tips for stovetop cooking:

- Keep pot and pan handles turned in toward the stove so that they don't get bumped accidentally in kitchen hustle and bustle.
- Some of these dishes can be served right out of the pot. Just be sure to place the hot pots on trivets to protect your counters and tabletops.
- Use a spoon rest or a small plate near the stovetop or on the counter. It keeps your mixing spoons handy as well as making cleanup easier.

- Don't wear loose-fitting clothing or aprons while cooking. That makes it easier to keep out of direct contact with burners and/or flames.
- When heating oil for frying or sautéing, never leave it unattended.
- When frying and sautéing, it's a good idea to have your exhaust fan on to eliminate steam and lingering food odors.

Stovetop Favorites

Spicy Orange Beef 98

Stylish Beef Stroganoff 99

After-Work Pepper Steak 100

Mustard Steak 101

Southern Chicken-Fried Steak 102

Saucy Beef Stir-fry 103

Make-Ahead Fajitas 104

Beef 'n' Peppers 105

My Country-Fried Steak 106

Tonight's One-Skillet Steak 107

Melt-in-Your-Mouth Swiss Steak 108

Beef and Broccoli Stir-fry 109

Pork Piccata 110

Inviting Pork Tenderloin 111

Off-the-Vine Pork Loin 112

Shortcut Sausage and Beans 113

Possible Orchard Pork 114

Veal Francaise 115

Veal with Vodka Sauce 116

Harvest Garden Veal 118

Quick Veal Marsala 119

Spicy Orange Beef

* * *

4 servings

Why not serve this as part of a Chinese-style buffet? You could make this, Possible Orchard Pork (page 114), and your favorite fried rice. It'll be a breeze!

3 tablespoons peanut oil, divided
1 tablespoon soy sauce
1 teaspoon ground ginger
1/2 teaspoon sugar
1 to 1 1/2 pounds beef top or bottom round steak, cut into 2-inch strips
Peel of 1 orange, cut into 1/8-inch strips
2 tablespoons all-purpose flour
1/4 cup orange juice
1/4 teaspoon cayenne pepper
1/2 cup ready-to-use beef broth

STORE MEAT COVERED IN THE REFRIGERATOR BETWEEN 35°F. AND 40°F.

In a medium-sized bowl, combine 1 tablespoon peanut oil, the soy sauce, ginger, and sugar; mix well. Add the beef strips and toss to coat. Meanwhile, heat the remaining peanut oil in a large skillet or wok over medium heat. Add the orange peel to the skillet and sauté for 3 to 4 minutes, or until it begins to brown. Add the flour to the meat mixture and stir until well coated; place the beef in the skillet and cook for 5 to 7 minutes or until no pink remains, stirring occasionally. Add the orange juice, cayenne pepper, and beef broth. Stir well to mix any flour from the bottom of the pan. Reduce the heat to low and cook for 7 to 9 more minutes, or until the sauce is thickened.

Stylish Beef Stroganoff

* * *

4 servings

Lately our eating styles are saying "back to basics." What's more basic than a good old-fashioned beef stroganoff?

1 pound boneless beef tri-tip (bottom sirloin), cut into 1-inch chunks
1/4 teaspoon salt
1/8 teaspoon black pepper
1/2 pound mushrooms, cut into 1/2-inch slices (about 3 cups)
1 small onion, chopped
2 tablespoons all-purpose flour
3/4 cup ready-to-use beef broth
1/4 cup sour cream

In a large skillet that has been coated with nonstick vegetable spray, brown the beef with the salt and pepper over medium-high heat for 3 to 5 minutes, or until no pink remains. Remove the meat and all but 2 teaspoons of the pan juices to a medium-sized bowl; set aside. Sauté the mushrooms and onion for 4 to 5 minutes, or until tender. Stir in the flour, then add the broth, stirring constantly. Bring to a boil and cook for 2 minutes, or until the sauce has thickened. Return the beef and juices to the skillet and cook for 3 to 4 minutes, or until heated through. Serve with a dollop of sour cream over each serving.

NOTE: This is usually served over curly egg noodles. For extra color, sprinkle some chopped scallions over the top, too.

After-Work Pepper Steak

* * *

4 to 5 servings

This is the kind of dish we all need after especially hectic workdays. It teams our meat and veggies and cooks up fast on the stovetop.

- 1/2 cup ready-to-use beef broth
- 3 tablespoons soy sauce
- 1 tablespoon cornstarch
- 1 teaspoon ground ginger
- 2 tablespoons vegetable oil
- 1 to 1 1/2 pounds beef top or bottom round steak, cut into 1/2-inch strips
- 1 medium-sized red bell pepper, cut into 1/4-inch strips
- 4 ounces fresh mushrooms, sliced (about 1 2/3 cups)
- 3 scallions, sliced
- 1 garlic clove, minced

In a small bowl, combine the broth, soy sauce, cornstarch, and ginger; mix well and set aside. In a large skillet, heat the oil over medium-high heat and sauté the beef for 2 to 3 minutes, or until browned. Add the pepper, mushrooms, scallions, and garlic and cook for 4 to 5 more minutes, or until the vegetables are tender. Add the broth mixture to the skillet and cook for 2 to 3 more minutes, or until the sauce thickens.

NOTE: Red or green—even yellow, orange, or purple—bell peppers will do the trick here. You might have a different color on hand every time you make this. Use whatever you've got!

Mustard Steak

* * *

6 servings

Wake up your taste buds with this stovetop "quickie."

1½ to 2 pounds beef flank steak, 1 inch thick
3 tablespoons spicy brown mustard
2 tablespoons butter
⅓ cup dry white wine
2 teaspoons light or dark brown sugar
½ teaspoon salt

Using a sharp knife, score the beef, cutting a crisscross pattern on both sides of the steak about ⅛ inch deep. Spread 1 tablespoon mustard over each side of the steak. In a large skillet, melt the butter over medium-high heat. Cook the steak for 12 to 15 minutes, or until desired doneness, turning halfway through the cooking. Stir in the wine, brown sugar, salt, and the remaining mustard. Cook for 2 to 3 minutes, or until the sauce thickens slightly, turning the steak once during cooking. Thinly slice the steak across the grain and serve topped with the sauce.

Southern Chicken-Fried Steak

* * *

4 servings

You don't have to be from the South to enjoy this down-home favorite.

1/4 cup plus 2 tablespoons all-purpose flour, divided
2 1/2 teaspoons salt, divided
1 1/4 teaspoons black pepper, divided
1 to 1 1/4 pounds beef cubed steak
1 egg
2 1/4 cups milk, divided
1/2 cup dry bread crumbs
1 cup vegetable oil

In a shallow dish, combine 1/4 cup flour, 1/2 teaspoon salt, and 1/4 teaspoon pepper. Coat the steak in the flour mixture and set aside. In a medium-sized bowl, combine the egg and 1/4 cup milk; mix well. Place the bread crumbs in another shallow dish. Dip the coated steak into the egg mixture, coating completely, then into the bread crumbs; set aside. Discard any remaining coating mixture. In a large deep skillet, heat the oil over medium-high heat until hot but not smoking. Add the steak and cook for 6 to 8 minutes, or until the juices run clear and the coating is golden brown, turning occasionally. Place on a platter covered with paper towels and cover with aluminum foil to keep warm. Drain off all but 2 tablespoons of the oil. Stir in the remaining 2 tablespoons flour and brown over low heat. Add the remaining salt, pepper and milk, stirring constantly for 3 to 4 minutes, or until the mixture thickens into gravy. Place the meat on a serving platter and top with the gravy.

NOTE: If you want to give it some zip, add 1/2 teaspoon hot pepper sauce to the gravy.

Saucy Beef Stir-fry

* * *

4 to 6 servings

You know me—always trying new combinations of simple ingredients. What I've got for you now is a quick stir-fry with a creamier sauce than usual. I know I like the results. How 'bout you?

  1 tablespoon vegetable oil
  2 garlic cloves, minced
  1 1/2 to 2 pounds boneless beef top sirloin steak, cut into 1/2-inch
    strips
  1/4 cup tomato paste
  1 can (10 3/4 ounces) condensed cream of mushroom soup
  1 1/2 cups water
  1 teaspoon dried thyme
  1 teaspoon salt
  1/2 teaspoon black pepper
  1 teaspoon browning and seasoning sauce
  1 package (16 ounces) frozen Oriental-style vegetables, thawed and
    drained

USE OR FREEZE LEFTOVERS AS SOON AS POSSIBLE

In a large deep skillet or wok, heat the vegetable oil over medium-high heat and sauté the garlic for about 1 minute, or until it just begins to brown, stirring frequently. Add the beef and cook for 7 to 9 minutes, or until browned, stirring occasionally. In a medium-sized bowl, combine the remaining ingredients except the vegetables; mix well. Stir into the skillet and cook for 3 to 4 minutes, until the sauce begins to boil, stirring frequently. Add the vegetables and cook for 2 to 3 more minutes, until heated through.

NOTE: I like to serve this over hot cooked rice. And if you prefer, you can substitute 1/2 cup dry red wine for 1/2 cup water.

Make-Ahead Fajitas

* * *

10 fajitas

Sure, this is made partly on the range, but the great thing about these fajitas is that right before serving, you bake them in the oven so they're ready whenever your posse is ready.

3 tablespoons vegetable oil, divided
2 large onions, cut into 8 wedges each
1 large green bell pepper, cut into 1/2-inch strips
1 large red bell pepper, cut into 1/2-inch strips
1 pound beef flank steak, cut into thin strips
2 tablespoons dry fajita seasoning
Ten 7-inch flour tortillas
1 cup (4 ounces) shredded Cheddar cheese
1 cup sour cream
1 cup salsa

Preheat the oven to 350°F. In a large skillet, heat 2 tablespoons of the oil over medium-high heat. Add the onions and peppers and sauté for 10 to 12 minutes, or until the onions are lightly browned; place in a large bowl and set aside. Heat the remaining 1 tablespoon of oil in the skillet and add the flank steak. Add the fajita seasoning and sauté for 3 to 4 minutes, until the steak begins to brown. Return the vegetables to the skillet and cook for 3 to 4 more minutes, stirring occasionally. Divide the flank steak mixture equally among the tortillas and roll up. Place the roll-ups seam sides down in a 9" × 13" baking dish that has been coated with nonstick vegetable spray. Sprinkle with the cheese, loosely cover with aluminum foil, and bake for 15 to 20 minutes. Serve with the sour cream and salsa.

NOTE: To make these ahead of time, cover and chill them after filling and rolling. Then bake for 20 to 25 minutes at 350°F.

Beef 'n' Peppers

* * *

4 to 6 servings

The marinade is the secret to this recipe. The way these citrus and soy flavors "marry" with the meat tells us it's gonna be a winner every time!

1/3 cup soy sauce
Juice of 2 limes (about 1/4 cup)
3/4 cup orange juice
1 teaspoon garlic powder
1/2 teaspoon black pepper
2 tablespoons sugar
1 1/2 pounds beef top or bottom round steak, cut into 1/2-inch strips
2 medium-sized red or green bell peppers, cut into 1/2-inch strips
1/4 cup chopped shallots or onion
2 teaspoons cornstarch

In a medium-sized bowl, combine the soy sauce, lime juice, orange juice, garlic powder, black pepper, and sugar; mix until the sugar is dissolved. Place the beef into the marinade and toss to coat. Cover and chill for at least 4 hours, or overnight. Reserve 2/3 cup of the marinade and discard the remaining marinade. Coat a medium-sized skillet or a wok with nonstick vegetable spray and heat over medium-high heat. Cook the meat for 8 to 10 minutes, or until browned, stirring frequently. Add the bell peppers and shallots and cook for 4 to 6 more minutes, or until the peppers are just tender. Reduce the heat to medium. Add the cornstarch to the reserved marinade; mix well and slowly add to the skillet. Bring to a boil, stirring constantly. Cook for about 2 minutes, or until the liquid thickens and turns glossy.

NOTE: When I need a super-quick dinner, I serve this over hot cooked brown or white rice.

My Country-Fried Steak

* * *

4 servings

I first had country-fried steak years ago at a little southern diner. Boy, was I hooked! And once your gang gets a taste, it's gonna be "Move over, fried chicken" at your house!

1 tablespoon salt, divided
1 cup cold water
1 to 1½ pounds beef cubed steaks
1 cup all-purpose flour
¾ teaspoon black pepper, divided
1 cup vegetable oil
2 cups milk

In a medium-sized bowl, combine 1 teaspoon salt and the water; stir until the salt is dissolved. Add the steak and soak for 10 minutes. In a medium-sized bowl, combine the flour, 1 teaspoon salt, and ½ teaspoon pepper; mix well. Reserve 2 tablespoons of the mixture and set aside. Remove the steaks one at a time from the water and coat completely with the flour mixture. In a large deep skillet over medium-high heat, heat the oil until very hot, but not smoking. Carefully add the steaks to the skillet and fry for 12 to 15 minutes, or until the juices run clear and the coating is golden brown, turning occasionally. Remove the steaks to a covered serving platter and keep warm. Drain off all but 2 tablespoons of the oil. Add the reserved flour mixture to the skillet and brown lightly over medium-low heat. Add the remaining salt and pepper and the milk. Bring to a boil, stirring frequently. Reduce the heat to low and simmer for 3 to 5 minutes, or until thick and creamy. Serve the steaks topped with the gravy.

Tonight's One-Skillet Steak

* * *

4 servings

No marinating, no fancy ingredients, one skillet. Boy oh boy! This sure does sound perfect for tonight (or any night)!

1/3 cup all-purpose flour
1 teaspoon salt
1/2 teaspoon black pepper
1 1/4 to 1 1/2 pounds beef cubed steaks
3 tablespoons vegetable oil
1/3 cup mayonnaise
2 tablespoons balsamic vinegar
1 tablespoon Dijon-style mustard

KEEP RAW AND COOKED MEATS SEPARATED

In a shallow dish, combine the flour, salt, and pepper; mix well. Completely coat the steaks with the flour mixture. In a large skillet, heat the oil over medium-high heat and sauté the steaks for 6 to 8 minutes, until the juices run clear, turning once. Place the steaks on a covered serving platter. Drain the excess liquid from the skillet and reduce the heat to low. In a small bowl, whisk together the mayonnaise, vinegar, and mustard; add to the skillet. Return the cubed steaks to the skillet, coating completely with the mayonnaise mixture. Cook for 3 to 4 minutes, or until heated through.

NOTE: You might want to use Dijon-style mustard one time and another time try one of the many mustard blends that are now available.

Melt-in-Your-Mouth Swiss Steak

* * *

4 to 5 servings

It's always nice when you can turn less-expensive meat cuts into quick-cooking dishes that even taste fancy. Here's a perfect example...

- ½ cup all-purpose flour
- 1 teaspoon salt
- ½ teaspoon black pepper
- 2 to 2½ pounds beef cubed steaks
- ¼ cup plus 2 tablespoons vegetable oil, divided
- ¾ cup chopped celery (2 to 3 stalks)
- 1 small onion, chopped
- 1 can (14½ ounces) sliced carrots, drained
- 1 jar (28 ounces) spaghetti sauce

In a shallow bowl, combine the flour, salt, and pepper; completely coat the steaks with the mixture. In a large skillet, heat the ¼ cup oil over medium-high heat; add the steaks and cook for 6 to 8 minutes, turning halfway through the cooking. Remove the steaks from the skillet and set aside. Heat the remaining oil in the skillet over medium-high heat and sauté the celery and onion for 5 minutes, or until tender. Add the carrots and spaghetti sauce; mix well. Add the steaks to the mixture, reduce the heat to low, and simmer for 10 to 12 minutes, or until the steaks are cooked through.

Beef and Broccoli Stir-fry

* * *

4 to 5 servings

You won't believe how far a pound of beef will go when served in this stir-fry. And with some fried or plain cooked rice, the only thing your group will need is their fortune cookies for dessert!

FOR A LEANER FINISHED DISH,
TRIM EXCESS FAT BEFORE COOKING

- ³/₄ cup ready-to-use beef broth
- 1 tablespoon soy sauce
- 1 teaspoon garlic powder
- ¹/₂ teaspoon ground ginger
- ¹/₂ teaspoon black pepper
- 2 tablespoons light or dark brown sugar
- 1 tablespoon cornstarch
- 1 to 1¹/₂ pounds beef top or bottom round steak, cut into ¹/₄-inch julienne strips
- 1 medium-sized onion, cut into ¹/₂-inch wedges
- ¹/₂ of a head of broccoli, cut into florets

In a small bowl, combine the beef broth, soy sauce, garlic powder, ginger, pepper, brown sugar, and cornstarch; mix well and set aside. In a large skillet or wok that has been coated with nonstick vegetable spray, brown the beef over medium-high heat for 5 minutes, stirring frequently. Add the onion and broccoli and cook for 3 to 4 minutes, or until the onion is tender and no pink remains in the beef. Add the beef broth mixture to the skillet and stir constantly for 2 to 3 minutes, or until the sauce begins to thicken. Remove from the heat and cover for 2 minutes, or until the broccoli is tender but still bright green.

Pork Piccata

* * *

6 servings

I used to shy away from a recipe if I was intimidated by its name! But after I decided to try a few of them anyway, and found out how good they were, I came up with some shortcuts so that we could all enjoy dishes like this.

1 to 1¹/₂ pounds boneless center-cut single pork loin, cut into
     ¹/₂-inch-thick slices
1¹/₄ cups half-and-half, divided
¹/₃ cup all-purpose flour
¹/₄ teaspoon white pepper
¹/₄ teaspoon paprika
1 to 2 tablespoons butter, divided
¹/₄ cup dry white wine
1 tablespoon lemon juice
¹/₂ teaspoon dried thyme
¹/₂ teaspoon salt

Lay each pork loin slice between 2 sheets of plastic wrap and pound with a kitchen mallet or rolling pin to ¹/₄-inch thickness. Place ²/₃ cup half-and-half in a shallow dish and set aside. In another shallow dish, combine the flour, pepper, and paprika; set aside. Heat 1 tablespoon butter in a large skillet over medium-high heat. Completely coat the pork with the half-and-half, then with the flour mixture. Cook for 4 to 6 minutes per side, until golden brown. Remove the pork to a covered platter to keep warm. If necessary, repeat the process using the remaining butter until all the pork is cooked, and set aside. Add the wine, lemon juice, thyme, and salt to the skillet and cook for 3 minutes over medium-low heat. Add the remaining half-and-half and reduce the heat to low. Return the pork to the skillet and simmer for 3 to 4 minutes, until thoroughly heated and the sauce is creamy.

Inviting Pork Tenderloin

* * *

3 to 4 servings

The flavor of oranges with a hint of nutmeg sure is inviting. It definitely invites second helpings!

   1 to 1½ pounds pork tenderloin (2 tenderloins)
   ¾ teaspoon salt
   ½ teaspoon paprika
   2 tablespoons vegetable oil
   ½ cup orange juice
   ¼ teaspoon ground nutmeg
   1 tablespoon light or dark brown sugar
   1 tablespoon orange marmalade
   1 can (11 ounces) mandarin oranges, drained and juice reserved
   2 teaspoons cornstarch

Sprinkle the pork with the salt and paprika; set aside. In a large deep skillet, heat the oil over medium heat until very hot but not smoking. Add the pork and cook for 5 to 6 minutes, turning occasionally until evenly browned. Add the orange juice, nutmeg, brown sugar, and marmalade. Reduce the heat to medium-low, cover, and cook for 25 to 30 minutes, or until cooked through, turning once after 15 minutes. In a small bowl, combine the reserved mandarin orange juice and the cornstarch; add to the skillet and stir until well mixed. Cook for 3 to 4 more minutes and remove from the heat. Slice across the grain and serve topped with the sauce and mandarin oranges.

NOTE: Pork tenderloin is often confused with pork loin. Don't be afraid to ask your butcher so you can be sure to get the right one.

Off-the-Vine Pork Loin

✳ ✳ ✳

4 to 5 servings

No, the pork really isn't "off the vine," but the taste sure is. That's because of the grapes and the grape juice. Fortunately, unlike great wine, this recipe takes no time at all.

> 1½ to 2 pounds boneless center-cut single pork loin, trimmed and cut into ½-inch-thick slices
> ⅓ cup all-purpose flour
> 2 tablespoons olive oil, plus more if needed
> ½ pound seedless white grapes, halved (about 1½ cups)
> ½ teaspoon dried thyme
> 1 tablespoon light or dark brown sugar
> 1¼ cups white grape juice
> ¼ teaspoon salt

Lay the pork slices between 2 sheets of plastic wrap and pound with a mallet or rolling pin to ¼-inch thickness. Place the flour in a shallow dish and coat the cutlets lightly with the flour. In a large skillet, heat 2 tablespoons oil over medium-high heat. Carefully place the pork in the hot oil. Sauté for 4 to 5 minutes per side, or until golden brown. Remove the pork to a covered platter and add more oil to the skillet if needed to finish cooking all of the cutlets. Add the remaining ingredients to the skillet and bring to a boil over medium heat. Reduce the heat to low and return the cutlets to the skillet. Simmer for 3 to 4 minutes, until the sauce begins to thicken. Serve the cutlets topped with the sauce.

NOTE: If you'd like an even more intense "off-the-vine" flavor, you can replace half the grape juice with dry white wine.

Shortcut Sausage and Beans

* * *

5 to 6 servings

I know, I know—you want the taste of the one-pot dish that Mama used to make, but you don't have time to cook it all day. Well, by using canned beans, we can take a shortcut that lets us serve this up in minutes.

   1 pound sweet or hot Italian sausage, casings removed
   1 medium-sized onion, thinly sliced
   2 garlic cloves, minced
   1 can (14½ ounces) stewed tomatoes
   1 tablespoon light or dark brown sugar
   ½ teaspoon dried rosemary
   ½ teaspoon dried oregano
   ½ teaspoon dried thyme
   1 can (15 ounces) cannellini beans (white kidney beans), drained
   1 can (15 ounces) garbanzo beans (chick peas), drained

In a soup pot, sauté the sausage over medium-high heat for about 1 minute. Add the onion and garlic and cook for 6 to 8 minutes, or until no pink remains in the sausage, stirring to crumble the sausage. Add the remaining ingredients and cook for 20 more minutes, stirring occasionally.

NOTE: A loaf of crusty bread is the perfect go-along.

Possible Orchard Pork

* * *

4 to 5 servings

Think it's impossible? No apples to core, peel, or slice, but still the fresh taste of the orchard shines through. How? Just look at the last ingredient . . . that's what makes it possible.

1 to 1½ pounds boneless center-cut pork loin, cut into ¼-inch
    julienne strips
2 medium-sized green or red bell peppers, cut into ½-inch strips
1 medium-sized onion, cut into ½-inch strips
½ of a head of broccoli, cut into florets
½ cup teriyaki sauce
2 tablespoons honey
½ teaspoon ground nutmeg
1 cup chunky-style applesauce

In a large skillet or wok that has been coated with nonstick vegetable spray, brown the pork over medium-high heat for 4 to 6 minutes, stirring frequently. Add the peppers, onion, and broccoli. Cook for 3 to 4 minutes, or until no pink remains in the pork. In a small bowl, combine the remaining ingredients; mix well. Reduce the heat to medium and add the applesauce mixture to the skillet. Toss to coat the pork and cook for 2 to 3 more minutes, or until the sauce begins to thicken.

NOTE: For an extra-special taste, sprinkle ¼ cup chopped pecans over the top before serving. And you can give it a festive look by using 1 red and 1 green bell pepper.

Veal Francaise

* * *

4 to 5 servings

Don't let the fancy name scare you. Sure, this tastes fancy, but it's really a snap to make. If you don't believe me, try it and see for yourself.

  1/2 cup all-purpose flour
  1/2 teaspoon salt
  3 eggs, lightly beaten
  3 tablespoons butter, plus more if needed
  1 to 1 1/4 pounds veal cutlets, pounded to 1/4-inch thickness
  1/3 cup dry white wine or dry vermouth
  Juice of 1 lemon (2 to 3 tablespoons)

In a shallow dish, combine the flour and salt; mix well. Beat the eggs in another shallow dish. In a large skillet, melt 3 tablespoons butter over medium heat. Coat the veal in the flour, then in the eggs. Cook the veal for 2 to 3 minutes per side, or until golden. If necessary, cook the veal in more than 1 batch, removing the cooked butter and adding more if necessary. Return all of the cooked veal to the skillet. Add the wine and squeeze the lemon over the veal. Cook for 2 to 3 more minutes, or until the sauce begins to glaze and thickens slightly.

NOTE: Wanna give this an extra lemony zing? Go ahead and add a bit more lemon juice. Remember, what counts is that you give it the tastes *you* like!

STORE MEAT COVERED IN THE REFRIGERATOR BETWEEN 35°F. AND 40°F.

Veal with Vodka Sauce

* * *

4 to 5 servings

If you're planning a special dinner for company, I've got your main dish recipe right here! Mmm...tender veal and incredible vodka sauce.

1/2 cup all-purpose flour
2 teaspoons salt, divided
1/4 cup (1/2 stick) butter, divided
1 to 1 1/4 pounds veal cutlets, pounded to 1/4-inch thickness
2 tablespoons olive oil
1 small onion, finely chopped
1 cup canned crushed tomatoes
1/2 cup heavy cream
1 teaspoon black pepper
1/3 cup vodka

In a shallow dish, combine the flour and 1 teaspoon salt; mix well. In a large skillet, melt 2 tablespoons butter over medium-high heat. Completely coat the veal in the flour mixture; sauté the cutlets for about 2 minutes per side, or until lightly browned. If necessary, sauté the veal in more than 1 batch. Remove the cooked veal to a covered platter to keep warm. Heat the oil and melt the remaining butter in the skillet over medium heat. Add the onion and sauté for 2 minutes, just until the onion is tender. Add the tomatoes, cream, pepper, and remaining salt. Cook for 1 minute, stirring occasionally. Add the vodka and cook for 2 more minutes, or until the vodka evaporates slightly and the sauce thickens, stirring occasionally. Add the veal to the simmering vodka sauce and continue simmering for 3 to 4 minutes, or until the veal is heated through. Serve immediately.

NOTE: Oh! I mentioned company. That's because when company is expected, it usually works out better if you've made something ahead of time. This one works because it just needs reheating. So when your company gets there, simply reheat it over low heat until it's warm. And to give it a special touch, you might want to drain and quarter one 14-ounce can artichoke hearts and add those along with the vodka.

Harvest Garden Veal

* * *

4 to 6 servings

Our summer gardens give us an abundance of plump plum tomatoes and a never-ending supply of fresh basil, so why not team them in a yummy veal cutlet recipe? I have! (And with today's super produce availability, it can become a year-round favorite.)

 ¹/₃ cup all-purpose flour
 1 teaspoon salt, divided
 ¹/₂ teaspoon black pepper, divided
 1 to 1¹/₄ pounds veal cutlets, pounded to ¹/₄-inch thickness
 ¹/₄ cup olive oil
 3 garlic cloves, minced
 3 plum tomatoes, coarsely chopped
 2 tablespoons chopped fresh basil
 ¹/₂ cup dry white wine or chicken broth

In a shallow pan, combine the flour, ¹/₂ teaspoon salt, and ¹/₄ teaspoon pepper; mix well. Completely coat the veal with the flour mixture. In a large skillet, heat the oil over medium heat. Add the garlic and sauté until golden. Add half of the veal and sauté for 4 to 5 minutes, or until the veal is lightly browned, turning once. Remove to a covered serving platter and repeat with the remaining veal. Add the tomatoes and basil to the skillet and sauté for 1 to 2 minutes, or until the tomatoes soften slightly. Add the wine and the remaining salt and pepper. Return the veal to the skillet and cook for 3 to 4 minutes, until the sauce has thickened and the veal is heated through.

NOTE: Bottled chopped garlic is a nice alternative to minced fresh garlic cloves, so why not keep a jar on hand? It's just one more way to keep things simple.

Quick Veal Marsala

* * *

4 to 5 servings

You thought tasty and easy couldn't be in the same recipe? This one proves that they can.

    1/2 cup all-purpose flour
    1 teaspoon salt
    1/4 teaspoon black pepper
    1 to 1 1/4 pounds veal cutlets, pounded to 1/4-inch thickness
    3 tablespoons butter
    3 tablespoons olive oil
    1/2 pound fresh mushrooms, sliced (about 3 cups)
    3/4 cup Marsala or other dry red wine

In a shallow dish, combine the flour, salt, and pepper. Coat the veal with the flour mixture and set aside. In a large skillet, melt the butter over medium heat and add the oil. Sauté the veal for 5 to 7 minutes, or until browned, turning once. (Cook the veal in more than 1 batch, if necessary.) Remove the cooked veal to a platter and keep warm. Sauté the mushrooms in the skillet for 4 to 5 minutes, or until tender. Return the veal to the skillet, add the wine, reduce the heat to low, and cook for 3 to 4 more minutes, or until the sauce thickens and the veal is heated through.

NOTE: You're probably wondering why you need to sauté in both olive oil and butter. Well, butter won't burn if it's mixed with oil, so that's how we can still enjoy its great flavor.

Oven Easies

What a collection! From small roasts to pot pies and skewered favorites, these are quick and easy dishes that take no time to prepare. They get popped into the oven and seem to cook in no time. Your oven does all the work!

- It's best to cook with the oven rack in the center of the oven. The higher the rack, the quicker your food will brown.
- Always preheat your oven (unless otherwise directed).
- Be sure to check the calibration of your oven frequently. You can have a professional do this, or you can buy an inexpensive oven thermometer and do it yourself (see page xxvi).
- Don't overcrowd your oven. This will keep the heat from circulating evenly. Also, cooking a lot of items at the same time will increase the cooking time of each.
- Don't open your oven door excessively while cooking, because this will lower the oven temperature and increase your cooking time(s).

- If your "oven easy" gets a bit too brown before it's done, it's usually okay to cover it with aluminum foil. But remember, doing that traps the steam in and may make certain foods too wet. For example, you wouldn't want dishes like Steak Cobbler (page 128) and Mom's Beef Pot Pie (page 124) to get soggy, so cover them loosely, if necessary. But make sure to uncover the item for its last few minutes of cooking. You can also add a few slits to the foil to allow some steam to escape during cooking.

- You can use either the shiny or the dull side of aluminum foil against your food—there is no difference in how they work. Aluminum foil is metal and metal conducts electricity. Be careful when using aluminum foil around electrical outlets or appliances. Do not touch foil to anything electrical.

Oven Easies

Mom's Beef Pot Pie 124
Steak Florentine 126
Oven-Charred London Broil 127
Steak Cobbler 128
Individual Beef Wellington 130
Chilled Roasted Tenderloin 131
Spicy Beef with Black Bean Salsa 132
Sherry Mushroom Tenderloin 133
Zesty Salsa Kebabs 134
Garlic-Crusted Liver 135
Reuben Pizza 136
Hot Dog Tacos 137
Hula Skewers 138
Maple Pecan Pork 139
Company Pork Tenderloin 140
Honey-Dijon Pork Roast 141
Jamaican Pork Skewers 142
Island Breeze Pork 143
Bourbon Pork Tenderloin 144
Perfect Peachy Pork Tenderloin 145
Lamb Kebabs 146

Mom's Beef Pot Pie

* * *

4 to 6 servings

This one sure brings back lots of memories, doesn't it? Mom may have had no choice but to make homemade crust for *her* beef pot pie, but we can make ours without that much bother. And on a cold night, we can still feel the warm goodness in every bite.

  ³/₄ pound beef top or bottom round, cut into 1-inch cubes
  1 small onion, chopped
  2 tablespoons all-purpose flour
  ¹/₂ teaspoon salt
  ¹/₄ teaspoon black pepper
  1 tablespoon vegetable oil
  1 medium-sized potato, peeled and cut into ¹/₂-inch cubes
  1 package (10 ounces) frozen mixed vegetables, thawed and drained
  1 can (10¹/₂ ounces) condensed beef broth
  1 package (8 ounces) refrigerated crescent rolls (8 rolls)

Preheat the oven to 375°F. In a medium-sized bowl, combine the beef, onion, flour, salt, and pepper; mix well. Heat the oil in a large deep skillet over medium-high heat. Place the beef mixture in the skillet and cook for 3 to 5 minutes, or until no pink remains, stirring frequently. Add the potato and mixed vegetables to the skillet and cook for 5 minutes. Add the broth and bring to a boil. Reduce the heat to medium and cook for 10 to 12 minutes, or until the potatoes are tender and the liquid has thickened. Pour the beef mixture into a 9-inch pie pan that has been coated with nonstick vegetable spray. Separate the crescent rolls into 8 dough triangles. Starting from the wide end, roll up each triangle halfway. Place the triangles over the beef mixture with the wide ends touching the outside rim of the pie pan and the pointed ends touching in the center. Bake for 16 to 18 minutes, or until the crust is golden brown.

Steak Florentine

* * *

4 to 6 servings

Sounds fancy...looks fancy...but it's so easy! Of course, you could let your guests believe this took you all day. (It tastes like it!)

- 1 package (10 ounces) frozen chopped spinach, thawed and squeezed dry
- 1 can (2.8 ounces) French-fried onions
- $3/4$ cup (3 ounces) shredded Monterey Jack cheese
- $1/2$ teaspoon salt
- 4 to 6 beef cubed steaks ($1^1/2$ to $1^3/4$ pounds total), pounded to $1/4$-inch thickness
- 2 to 3 teaspoons Dijon-style mustard, divided
- 1 tablespoon olive oil
- $1/2$ teaspoon garlic powder
- $1/2$ teaspoon paprika
- $1/2$ teaspoon black pepper

Preheat the oven to 375°F. In a medium-sized bowl, combine the spinach, onions, cheese, and salt. Spread each cubed steak with $1/2$ teaspoon mustard. Spread the spinach mixture evenly over the tops of the steaks. Roll up each steak from a short end, tucking in the sides while rolling. In a small bowl, combine the olive oil, garlic powder, paprika, and pepper; mix well, then brush over the steak rolls. Place the steak rolls in a 9" × 13" baking dish that has been coated with non-stick vegetable spray. Bake for 45 to 50 minutes, or until the steaks are cooked, no pink remains, and the filling is hot. Cut into $1/2$-inch-thick slices and serve.

NOTE: For added flavor, serve with warm spaghetti sauce spooned over the steak.

Oven-Charred London Broil

* * *

4 to 5 servings

The charcoal seasoning makes this black on the outside, but it's still juicy on the inside—without a grill!

  2 tablespoons charcoal seasoning or steak seasoning
  One 1³/₄- to 2-pound beef top round steak or London broil

Preheat the oven to 400°F. Rub the charcoal seasoning or steak seasoning over the entire steak. Place on a cookie sheet and roast for 20 to 25 minutes for medium-rare, or until desired doneness. Cut across the grain into thin slices and serve.

NOTE: This is a great way to get barbecue taste without lighting the barbecue.

BE SURE TO DISCARD ANY EXCESS SEASONING MIX THAT HAS COME IN CONTACT WITH RAW MEAT!

Steak Cobbler

* * *

6 to 8 servings

Most people know about apple cobbler and cherry cobbler. Well, now there's steak cobbler, a quick main dish that'll get the same raves as the other cobblers.

1/3 cup all-purpose flour
2 teaspoons salt, divided
1/2 teaspoon black pepper
1 1/2 to 2 pounds beef top or bottom round, cut into 1/2-inch cubes
1/4 cup plus 2 tablespoons vegetable oil
2 medium-sized onions, cut into 1-inch wedges
1/2 pound fresh mushrooms, sliced (about 3 cups)
1 package (10 ounces) frozen mixed vegetables
1 cup ready-to-use beef broth
1/2 teaspoon garlic powder
1/4 teaspoon cayenne pepper
1 package (10 ounces) refrigerated buttermilk biscuits (12 biscuits)
1 package (4.5 ounces) refrigerated buttermilk biscuits (6 biscuits)

Preheat the oven to 375°F. In a medium-sized bowl, combine the flour, 1 teaspoon salt, and the black pepper; mix well. Add the beef cubes and toss until well coated. In a large skillet, heat the 2 tablespoons oil over medium-high heat. Add the beef cubes, reserving the flour mixture. Sauté for 3 to 4 minutes, or until the beef is slightly browned. Add the remaining oil to the skillet; when hot, add the onions and mushrooms and sauté for 4 to 5 minutes, or until the vegetables are tender. Add the remaining ingredients except the biscuits and cook for 3 to 4 minutes, or until heated through. Stir in the reserved flour mixture and cook for 1 to 2 more minutes, or until slightly thickened. Pour the beef mixture into a 2- or 2$\frac{1}{2}$-quart casserole dish that has been coated with nonstick vegetable spray. Place the biscuits over the meat mixture, completely covering the top. Bake for 16 to 18 minutes, or until the biscuits are golden brown.

Individual Beef Wellington

* * *

4 servings

People often assume that I always eat fancy dinners at home. I have a friend who used to kid around and say, "What are you having for dinner tonight: Beef Wellington?" Well, that was because he thought it was a really complicated dish. I took it as a challenge, so now, in about 30 minutes, we can all have the most elegant beef dinner. . . no kidding!

> 4 ounces fresh mushrooms, chopped (about 1 1/2 cups)
> 1 garlic clove, minced
> 1 package (17 1/4 ounces) frozen puff pastry dough, thawed
> 1/2 teaspoon salt
> 1/4 teaspoon black pepper
> 4 beef tenderloin fillet steaks (4 to 5 ounces each), 1 inch thick

Preheat the oven to 425°F. Place the mushrooms and garlic in a medium-sized nonstick skillet and cook over medium heat for 3 to 4 minutes, or until the mushrooms are tender. Remove from the heat, drain well, and set aside. Unfold the pastry sheets and cut each in half crosswise. Spoon the cooked mushrooms onto the center of each of the 4 pieces of pastry. Sprinkle the salt and pepper over both sides of the steaks and place the steaks over the mushrooms. Bring the corners of the pastry up over the steaks. Pinch the top corners and side edges together with your fingers to seal completely. Place in a 9" × 13" baking dish that has been coated with nonstick vegetable spray and bake for 20 to 25 minutes, or until the pastry is puffed and golden and the meat is cooked to medium-rare, or to desired doneness.

THOROUGHLY
WASH HANDS
OR ANY ITEMS
IMMEDIATELY
AFTER CONTACT WITH
RAW MEAT

Chilled Roasted Tenderloin

* * *

5 to 6 servings

Roasted tenderloin so tender it melts in your mouth...? Sure, it's a little more expensive, but don't you deserve it once in a while?

    2 to 2¹/₂ pounds beef tenderloin, trimmed
    1 tablespoon vegetable oil
    ¹/₂ teaspoon garlic powder
    ¹/₄ teaspoon black pepper
    6 hard rolls

Preheat the oven to 350°F. Place the tenderloin on a large rimmed cookie sheet that has been coated with nonstick vegetable spray. In a small bowl, combine the remaining ingredients except the rolls and rub the mixture over the entire roast. Cook for 35 to 40 minutes for medium-rare, or until desired doneness. Thinly slice the meat across the grain. Cover and chill for at least 2 hours. Serve cold on the rolls topped with Horseradish Sauce (page 16).

NOTE: A whole tenderloin of beef usually weighs between 4 and 7 pounds, but you can usually ask the butcher to cut a piece as large or as small as you need.

Spicy Beef with Black Bean Salsa

* * *

6 to 8 servings

Stop! If you've been looking for something different, you've found it! This is a spicy steak that's balanced by the cooling flavors of black bean salsa.

- 1 tablespoon chili powder
- 1 teaspoon ground cumin
- 1 teaspoon salt
- $\frac{1}{2}$ teaspoon cayenne pepper
- One 2- to $2\frac{1}{2}$-pound beef tri-tip roast or 1 boneless beef top sirloin steak, $1\frac{1}{2}$ inches thick
- 1 can (15 ounces) black beans, rinsed and drained
- 1 medium-sized tomato, chopped
- $\frac{1}{2}$ of a medium-sized red onion, chopped
- 3 tablespoons coarsely chopped fresh cilantro or parsley

Preheat the broiler. In a small bowl, combine the chili powder, cumin, salt, and cayenne pepper; mix well and set aside 2 teaspoons of the mixture. Rub the remaining mixture evenly over the entire surface of the meat. Broil for 25 to 30 minutes for medium-rare to medium, or until desired doneness, turning once during the broiling. Meanwhile, in a medium-sized bowl, combine the remaining ingredients, including the reserved 2 teaspoons seasoning mixture; mix well. Thinly slice the meat across the grain and serve with the bean salsa.

NOTE: I like to make the black bean salsa ahead of time and refrigerate it to allow the flavors to blend well. Then I serve the cold salsa with the warm meat for knockout flavor!

Sherry Mushroom Tenderloin

* * *

6 to 8 servings

Ooh-la-la! This may taste like it's from an expensive, fancy restaurant, but it's not. You'll be amazed by how easy it is to make a dinner that tastes this scrumptious!

3 tablespoons vegetable oil, divided
1 teaspoon salt
1/2 teaspoon garlic powder
1/2 teaspoon onion powder
1/4 teaspoon black pepper
2 to 2 1/2 pounds beef tenderloin, trimmed
1/2 pound fresh mushrooms, sliced (about 3 cups)
1 jar (12 ounces) brown gravy
1/2 teaspoon dried thyme
2 tablespoons cream sherry or sweet white wine

> FOR A LEANER FINISHED DISH,
> TRIM EXCESS FAT BEFORE COOKING

Preheat the oven to 450°F. In a small bowl, combine 2 tablespoons of the oil, the salt, garlic and onion powders, and black pepper; mix well. Rub the mixture over the entire tenderloin and place in a large roasting pan that has been coated with nonstick vegetable spray. Roast for 10 minutes, then reduce the heat to 350°F. and roast for 35 to 40 more minutes, or until a meat thermometer registers 140°F. for medium-rare, or to desired doneness beyond that. While the meat is cooking, heat the remaining oil in a large skillet over medium-high heat and sauté the mushrooms for 2 to 3 minutes, or until tender. Reduce the heat to low and stir in the gravy. Add the thyme and sherry and cook for 8 to 10 minutes, stirring occasionally. Slice the tenderloin and serve with the sherry sauce.

Zesty Salsa Kebabs

* * *

10 skewers

These have to marinate overnight, but boy, they're worth the wait. They've got such great spicy flavor!

1 jar (16 ounces) medium salsa
1/2 cup vegetable oil
1 teaspoon salt
1/2 cup dry white wine
2 pounds boneless beef chuck, cut into 1-inch cubes
2 medium-sized green bell peppers, cut into 1-inch chunks
1 medium-sized yellow or red bell pepper, cut into 1-inch chunks
1 medium-sized red onion, cut into 1-inch chunks
Ten 10-inch metal or bamboo skewers

In a medium-sized bowl, whisk together the salsa, oil, salt, and wine until well mixed; set aside. Alternately thread 4 pieces each of beef, green peppers, yellow peppers, and onion on each skewer. Lay the skewers in a shallow dish and cover completely with the salsa mixture. Cover and chill for 8 to 10 hours or overnight, turning the skewers occasionally. Preheat the broiler. Place the kebabs on a rimmed cookie sheet that has been covered with aluminum foil and coated with nonstick vegetable spray. Discard any excess marinade. Broil for 18 to 20 minutes for medium, or until desired doneness beyond that, turning the skewers halfway through the cooking.

NOTE: Go ahead! Serve these over hot cooked rice.

Garlic-Crusted Liver

* * *

4 to 6 servings

So good and full of garlic flavor they won't even know it's liver. I can keep a secret if you can!

    4 beef or calf's liver steaks (1½ to 2 pounds total)
    ¼ cup seasoned bread crumbs
    4 large garlic cloves, finely chopped
    ¼ teaspoon salt
    ¼ teaspoon black pepper
    1 tablespoon dried parsley flakes
    Nonstick vegetable spray

Preheat the oven to 400°F. Place the liver in a 9" × 13" baking dish that has been coated with nonstick vegetable spray. In a small bowl, combine the remaining ingredients and sprinkle over the steaks. Spray the steaks with vegetable spray and bake for 20 minutes, or until desired doneness.

NOTE: Beef and calf's livers do not have to be cooked until they're dry and hard. Try cooking them to medium-well so they're still moist and flavorful.

Reuben Pizza

* * *

6 to 8 slices

All the special tastes of a Reuben sandwich, with the ease of eating a slice of pizza. Now, that's an improvement on a classic!

One 12- to 14-inch (16-ounce) prepared pizza shell, thawed if frozen
1 can (14.4 ounces) sauerkraut, drained and squeezed dry
6 ounces sliced corned beef, cut into 1/2-inch strips
1/2 cup Russian dressing
1 cup (4 ounces) shredded Swiss cheese

Preheat the oven to 450°F. Place the pizza shell on a pan and sprinkle with the sauerkraut; set aside. In a small bowl, combine the corned beef and dressing; toss to coat. Spoon over the sauerkraut and top with the Swiss cheese. Bake for 12 to 14 minutes, or until the crust is crisp and brown. Cut and serve.

STORE MEAT COVERED IN THE REFRIGERATOR BETWEEN 35°F. AND 40°F.

Hot Dog Tacos

* * *

8 tacos

Hot dogs and tacos...two kids' favorites that are even better together. Won't they think you're clever?!

8 hot dogs
1 tablespoon dry taco seasoning mix
1 tablespoon vegetable oil
8 taco shells, slightly warmed
1 cup shredded iceberg lettuce
1 cup chopped tomatoes
1 cup (4 ounces) shredded Cheddar cheese

Preheat the barbecue grill to medium-high heat. Make a lengthwise slit almost (but not completely) through each hot dog. In a small bowl, combine the taco seasoning mix and the oil. Spread the mixture evenly into the slits in the hot dogs. Grill them cut side up for 5 to 7 minutes, then place each hot dog inside a warmed taco shell. Top with the lettuce, tomatoes, and cheese.

NOTE: You can make your own Taco Seasoning (page 89) for always having on hand, or simply use 1 tablespoon from a 1.25-ounce envelope of dry taco seasoning mix.

Hula Skewers

∗ ∗ ∗

8 skewers

I bet these make you feel like dancing the hula. Go ahead! And no, you won't need a grass skirt!

Eight 10-inch metal or bamboo skewers
1 cup prepared barbecue sauce
2 cans (8 ounces each) pineapple chunks, drained and 1/4 cup juice reserved
2 tablespoons orange marmalade
1/2 teaspoon garlic powder
1/2 teaspoon hot pepper sauce
2 medium-sized green bell peppers, cut into 16 pieces each
1 1/2 to 2 pounds boneless beef chuck, cut into 1-inch cubes

If using bamboo skewers, soak them in water for 15 to 20 minutes. Preheat the broiler. In a medium-sized bowl, combine the barbecue sauce, the reserved pineapple juice, the marmalade, garlic powder, and hot pepper sauce; mix well and set aside. Alternately thread each skewer with 4 pieces each of bell pepper, steak, and pineapple. Lay the skewers 1 inch apart on a broiler pan or rimmed cookie sheet that has been covered with aluminum foil that has been coated with non-stick vegetable spray. Generously baste all sides of the kebabs with the sauce. Broil for 14 to 16 minutes, or until the steak is cooked to desired doneness, turning halfway through the cooking.

NOTE: For a more complete meal, serve over hot cooked rice.

> FOR A LEANER FINISHED DISH,
> TRIM EXCESS FAT BEFORE COOKING

Maple Pecan Pork

* * *

3 to 4 servings

I got this idea while I was eating a pecan roll. I was thinking that it tasted so good I wished I could have it for dinner. Well, I think I succeeded in making a main course that tastes just as good! What do *you* think?

- 1/2 cup plus 2 tablespoons maple syrup
- 1/2 teaspoon lemon juice
- 3/4 teaspoon salt
- 1/4 teaspoon white pepper
- One 2- to 2 1/2-pound boneless center-cut single pork loin
- 1/2 cup chopped pecans

Preheat the oven to 350°F. In a small bowl, combine the maple syrup, lemon juice, salt, and pepper; mix well. Rub 2 tablespoons of the mixture over the entire pork loin. Press the pecans into the pork, coating all sides. Place the pork in a baking dish that has been coated with nonstick vegetable spray. Bake for 35 minutes. Remove the pork from the oven and pour the remaining syrup mixture over it. Bake for 10 to 15 more minutes, or until the juices run clear. Cut the pork into 1/2-inch slices and serve with the pan drippings.

NOTE: Walnuts are just as good as pecans here, or if you prefer, you can skip the nuts and make it just maple-flavored.

USE OR FREEZE LEFTOVERS AS SOON AS POSSIBLE

Company Pork Tenderloin

* * *

4 to 6 servings

Once you try this, I know you're gonna be looking for company to invite over!

  ½ cup bottled sweet-and-sour (duck) sauce
  1 tablespoon plus 1 teaspoon soy sauce
  ¼ teaspoon cayenne pepper
  1½ to 2 pounds pork tenderloin (2 tenderloins)

Preheat the oven to 400°F. In a small bowl, combine the sweet and sour sauce, soy sauce, and cayenne pepper; mix well. Place the pork on a rimmed cookie sheet that has been lined with aluminum foil and coated with nonstick vegetable spray. Spoon half the sauce over the pork and bake for 45 to 50 minutes, or until little pink remains for medium-well, or no pink remains for well-done. Slice the tenderloins into thin slices and serve topped with the remaining sauce.

Honey-Dijon Pork Roast

* * *

5 to 6 servings

In case you haven't figured it out yet, honey mustard is one of my favorite flavorings. Combining roasted pork with that winning combination really brings out the best of them *all*!

> ¼ cup honey
> 2 tablespoons plus 1 teaspoon Dijon-style mustard
> ½ teaspoon salt
> One 2- to 2¼-pound boneless center-cut single pork loin

Preheat the oven to 375°F. In a medium-sized bowl, combine the honey, mustard, and salt. Place the pork into a medium-sized roasting pan that has been coated with nonstick vegetable spray and coat completely with the mixture. Cover with aluminum foil and bake for 40 minutes. Uncover and baste with the pan drippings. Roast the pork for 15 to 20 more minutes, or until no pink remains. Slice and serve with the pan drippings.

NOTE: Thinly sliced and topped with a little extra Dijon-style mustard, this roast makes super sandwiches.

FOR A LEANER FINISHED DISH,
TRIM EXCESS FAT BEFORE COOKING

Jamaican Pork Skewers

* * *

10 skewers

Tropical breezes, beautiful waterfalls, and good food and drink. Isn't that what Jamaica is all about? Close your eyes, taste these, and let your imagination go!

- 1/2 cup vegetable oil
- 2 tablespoons bottled steak sauce
- 2 1/2 tablespoons light or dark brown sugar
- 1/3 cup creamy peanut butter
- 1 tablespoon soy sauce
- 1/4 cup shredded coconut
- 1/4 teaspoon garlic powder
- 1 1/4 to 1 1/2 pounds boneless center-cut single pork loin, cut into 1-inch cubes
- Ten 10-inch metal or bamboo skewers
- 1 apple, peeled, cored, and cut into 10 wedges
- 1 orange, peeled and cut into 10 chunks
- 2 kiwi, peeled and cut into 5 slices each

ALWAYS DISCARD USED MARINADE

In a blender, combine the oil, steak sauce, brown sugar, peanut butter, soy sauce, coconut, and garlic powder; blend thoroughly. Pour the mixture into a 9" × 13" glass baking dish and add the pork; toss to coat completely. Cover and chill for at least 2 hours, or overnight. If using bamboo skewers, soak them in water for 15 to 20 minutes. Preheat the broiler. Alternately thread the pork and fruit onto the skewers and place the skewers on a rimmed cookie sheet that has been covered with aluminum foil that has been coated with nonstick vegetable spray. Brush the remaining marinade over the skewers, then discard any excess marinade. Broil for 12 to 15 minutes, or until the pork is cooked through, turning once halfway through the cooking.

Island Breeze Pork

* * *

4 to 6 servings

Pineapple and coconut is such a classic "island" taste combination, so why not try it with pork? I think you'll agree that the classics just keep getting better and better!

> One 2- to 2½-pound boneless center-cut single pork loin
> 1 can (8 ounces) crushed pineapple, drained and juice reserved
> ½ cup shredded coconut
> 2 tablespoons light or dark rum
> Maraschino cherries for garnish

Preheat the oven to 350°F. Place the pork in a 9" × 13" baking dish that has been coated with nonstick vegetable spray. In a medium-sized bowl, combine the pineapple and coconut; mix well. Press the coconut mixture into the pork. In a small bowl, combine the pineapple juice and rum; pour over the pork. Garnish with the cherries. Bake for 55 to 60 minutes, until a meat thermometer registers 160°F. for medium-well, or until desired doneness beyond that. Cut the pork into ½-inch slices and serve with the pan drippings.

THOROUGHLY WASH HANDS OR ANY ITEMS IMMEDIATELY AFTER CONTACT WITH RAW MEAT

Bourbon Pork Tenderloin

* * *

4 to 5 servings

If you look at the first 3 ingredients, you might not know whether you're going to be frosting a cake or roasting a tenderloin. After just one bite of the finished dish you'll know that tenderloin was the right choice.

- 1 cup confectioners' sugar
- 2 tablespoons bourbon
- 1 teaspoon vanilla extract
- 1½ to 2 pounds pork tenderloin (2 tenderloins)
- ½ teaspoon salt
- ¼ teaspoon black pepper

Preheat the oven to 350°F. In a medium-sized bowl, combine the confectioners' sugar, bourbon, and vanilla; mix well and set aside. Sprinkle both sides of the pork with the salt and pepper, then place it in an 8-inch square baking dish that has been lined with aluminum foil and coated with nonstick vegetable spray. Pour half of the bourbon mixture over the pork and roast for 45 minutes. Remove the pork from the oven and pour the remaining sauce over it. Roast for 5 to 10 more minutes, or until no pink remains. Cut the tenderloins into ¼-inch slices and serve with the pan drippings.

NOTE: I line the pan with aluminum foil to make cleanup easy.

Perfect Peachy Pork Tenderloin

* * *

4 to 6 servings

Out of the orchards and onto your plate, this tenderloin is peachy... and perfect, too!

1½ to 2 pounds pork tenderloin (2 tenderloins)
1 can (16 ounces) peaches in heavy syrup, coarsely chopped
½ cup ketchup
¼ cup white vinegar
½ cup firmly packed dark brown sugar
1 tablespoon chili powder
1 teaspoon garlic powder
1 tablespoon salt

Preheat the oven to 350°F. Place the pork in a 9" × 13" baking dish that has been coated with nonstick vegetable spray; set aside. In a medium-sized saucepan, combine the remaining ingredients (including the peach syrup) and bring to a boil over medium heat. Pour the sauce mixture over the pork. Cover with aluminum foil and roast for 30 minutes. Reduce the heat to 325°F., uncover, and roast for 30 more minutes. Slice across the grain and serve with the sauce.

NOTE: The sauce has tons of flavor and it looks great over the pork, so don't skimp when serving it!

Lamb Kebabs

* * *

12 skewers

This marinade gives the lamb lots of flavor. And the kebabs cook in no time. Of course, that makes them the perfect addition to any outdoor grilling.

3 tablespoons vegetable oil
2 tablespoons lemon juice
1 teaspoon dried oregano
1/2 teaspoon garlic powder
1/4 teaspoon salt
1/8 teaspoon black pepper
1/8 teaspoon ground allspice
1 1/2 to 2 pounds lamb stew meat or boneless leg of lamb cut into
   1-inch pieces (about 36 pieces)
Twelve 10-inch metal or bamboo skewers
2 large red bell peppers, cut into 12 pieces each
1 large onion, halved and cut into 24 wedges

In a large bowl, combine the oil, lemon juice, oregano, garlic powder, salt, black pepper, and allspice; mix well. Add the lamb and toss to coat. Cover and chill for at least 4 to 6 hours, or overnight. If using bamboo skewers, soak them in water for 15 to 20 minutes. Preheat the broiler. Alternately skewer the lamb, bell pepper, and onion onto the skewers, so that there are 3 pieces of lamb, 2 pieces of bell pepper, and 2 pieces of onion on each skewer. Place the skewers on a broiler pan or cookie sheet that has been coated with nonstick vegetable spray and broil for 6 to 8 minutes. Turn the skewers over and broil for 5 to 6 more minutes, or until the lamb is cooked to medium, or to desired doneness beyond that. Serve immediately.

NOTE: These are great alone but I like to serve them on pita bread or over a simple rice pilaf . . . or both!

Worth the Wait

You know me—always looking for no-fuss solutions to cooking chores. Now, just because something cooks for a long time, that doesn't mean that it's difficult or takes a long time to prepare. Uh-uh! Here are some tips for helping you look like a kitchen hero by serving those luscious long-cooking meat cuts. There'll be no question at your house . . . they're definitely worth the wait!

- Line roasting pans with aluminum foil so that cleanup will be no hassle.
- Roast meats with the fat side up so that as the meat cooks, the fat will melt and flavor the meat.
- The lower the temperature, the longer the roasting time and the more evenly an item will cook. It's usually best to roast at a temperature between 325°F. and 400°F.
- Allow roasts to thaw before cooking. (See page xiv for proper defrosting information.)
- The best way to tell how much a roast is cooked is to use a meat thermometer (see page xxvi). (Also, see my roasting charts on pages xxi to xxv.)

- It's a good idea to let a roast stand or rest for 15 to 20 minutes after removing it from the oven, to allow the juices to settle and the cooking to stop.
- Carve roasts across the grain (see page xxviii).
- Sure, you can use your leftover roasts again and again. recommend heating them up in the pan juices or using them in other recipes. (See Soups, Salads, and Sandwiches, page 175.) With just one cooking, you'll get to enjoy the roast the same or different way(s) as a bonus!
- Large cuts of uncooked meat can be stored in the refrigerator for up to 1 week, or wrapped in aluminum foil and frozen for 8 to 9 months.

Worth the Wait

No-Roast Roast Brisket

* * *

6 to 8 servings

Wouldn't it be nice to have that big roasted taste without ever having to turn on your oven? Here's a perfect way to warm your tummy, not your kitchen!

2 teaspoons garlic powder
2 teaspoons onion powder
1½ teaspoons salt
1 teaspoon black pepper
1 tablespoon vegetable oil
1 medium-sized onion, chopped
One 2½- to 3-pound beef brisket
2 large ripe tomatoes, chopped
⅓ cup water

In a small bowl, combine the garlic powder, onion powder, salt, and pepper; mix well. In a large skillet, heat the oil over medium-high heat and sauté the onion for 4 to 5 minutes, until lightly browned. Meanwhile, sprinkle the seasoning mixture over both sides of the brisket. Place in the skillet and brown for 3 to 4 minutes per side. Add the tomatoes and water. Cover and reduce the heat to low; simmer for 2 ¾ to 3 hours, or until fork-tender. Remove the brisket from the skillet and cut across the grain into ¼-inch slices; return the slices to the pan. Cover and simmer for 10 more minutes, then serve with the sauce.

NOTE: This is even better rewarmed in its own juices the day after it's made.

Roast Prime Rib of Beef

* * *

8 to 10 servings

Sometimes the simplest things are the best. So why not enjoy your restaurant favorites at home—simply!

One 4- to 6-pound boneless beef rib eye or Delmonico roast
$^1/_2$ teaspoon garlic powder
$^1/_2$ teaspoon onion powder
1 tablespoon salt
$^1/_2$ teaspoon black pepper

Preheat the oven to 350°F. Place the meat fat side up in a large roasting pan that has been coated with nonstick vegetable spray. In a small bowl, combine the remaining ingredients; mix well. Rub the spice blend evenly over the surface of the meat. Place a meat thermometer so that the tip is centered in the roast but does not touch the fat. Roast the meat for 14 to 15 minutes per pound, or until the thermometer reaches 140°F. for medium-rare, or until the desired doneness. Remove the meat to a cutting board and let stand for 15 to 20 minutes before carving across the grain. Serve with the pan drippings.

NOTE: See my beef roasting guide on page xxi.

THOROUGHLY
WASH HANDS
OR ANY ITEMS
IMMEDIATELY
AFTER CONTACT WITH
RAW MEAT

Chinese Pot Roast

* * *

6 to 8 servings

Have you heard the old Chinese saying "It's better for a man to wait for food than for food to wait for a man"? Well, you're gonna think this dish is where it all started!

One 2- to 3-pound beef eye of the round roast, trimmed
1/3 cup vegetable oil
1/3 cup soy sauce
2 tablespoons lemon juice
2 tablespoons honey
1 garlic clove, minced
1 1/2 teaspoons ground ginger
2 medium-sized carrots, sliced 1/2 inch thick
1 small onion, quartered
1 package (16 ounces) frozen Oriental-style vegetables,
    thawed
2 tablespoons cornstarch

Place the roast in a resealable plastic storage bag and set it open end up in a deep bowl. In a small bowl, combine the oil, soy sauce, lemon juice, honey, garlic, and ginger; mix well. Pour into the bag and over the roast; seal the bag. Marinate in the refrigerator for 8 hours, or overnight, turning the bag occasionally to marinate evenly. Transfer the roast and the marinade to a soup pot. Cover and simmer over low heat for 1 hour. Add the carrots and onion and simmer for 1 1/2 hours, or until the meat and vegetables are tender. Slice the meat across the grain and place on a serving platter; cover to keep warm. In a medium-sized bowl, toss the stir-fry vegetables with the cornstarch;

add to the pan juices. Cook over medium-high heat, stirring, for 3 to 4 minutes, or until thickened and bubbly. Serve the sauce and vegetables over the sliced roast.

NOTE: With a bowl of fried rice, you've got yourself a meal-in-one that'll do a lot for your yen!

FOR A LEANER FINISHED DISH,
TRIM EXCESS FAT BEFORE COOKING

Savory Prime Rib

★ ★ ★

12 to 14 servings

Sure, this book is full of great recipes, but one of my favorites is right here. (I bet after you taste it it'll become one of your favorites, too!)

One 4- to 4½-pound beef rib eye roast
5 garlic cloves, minced
1½ teaspoons salt
1½ teaspoons black pepper
1½ teaspoons dried thyme
¾ teaspoon ground dried tarragon
1 jar (10 to 12 ounces) brown gravy
¼ cup dry red wine

Preheat the oven to 350°F. Place the roast fat side up in a large roasting pan that has been coated with nonstick vegetable spray. In a small bowl, combine the garlic, salt, pepper, thyme, and tarragon; mix well, then reserve 2 teaspoons of the mixture. Rub all but the reserved spice mixture evenly over the roast and roast for 1¼ to 1½ hours for medium-rare (150°F. on a meat thermometer), or until desired doneness. Remove from the oven and allow to stand for 10 minutes before cutting. In a medium-sized saucepan, heat the brown gravy, red wine, reserved spice mixture, and pan drippings over medium-low heat for 8 to 10 minutes, or until heated through, mixing well. Slice the rib eye across the grain and serve with the sauce.

NOTE: Nothing goes better with prime rib than baked potatoes, and since the oven is already on to make the roast, making the potatoes is easy as 1–2–3.

Old-Fashioned Deli Roast Beef

* * *

About 3 pounds cooked roast beef

You know that slow-cooked taste that really great deli roast beef has? Now you can get that at home—and for a lot less money, too! (You won't believe how easy it is!)

One 3- to 4-pound beef bottom round roast
$1/2$ teaspoon salt
$1/2$ teaspoon black pepper
$1/2$ teaspoon garlic powder
$1/2$ teaspoon onion powder
1 teaspoon paprika

Preheat the oven to 350°F. Place the roast fat side up on a roasting rack that has been coated with nonstick vegetable spray. Place the rack in a large roasting pan. In a small bowl, combine the remaining ingredients; mix well. Rub the spice mixture over the entire roast, covering completely. Roast for $1^1/4$ to $1^1/2$ hours, or until a meat thermometer registers 150°F. for medium-rare, or until desired doneness beyond that.

NOTE: This roast beef is perfect for French Double Dippers (page 191) and Philadelphia Cheese Steak Sandwiches (page 194). It will keep in the fridge for 3 or 4 days, so slice it very thin as you need it. You can also freeze it in 1-pound packages for future use.

Simmering Steak and Veggies

* * *

5 to 6 servings

"Simmering" means cooking over low heat. In this recipe, simmering means lots of long-cooked flavor and tenderness.

2 tablespoons vegetable oil
2½ to 3 pounds beef chuck steak (see Note)
1 can (15 ounces) tomato sauce
1 cup water
½ teaspoon ground allspice
2 teaspoons salt
1 teaspoon black pepper
6 medium-sized white potatoes, peeled and sliced about ¼ inch thick
3 medium-sized tomatoes, sliced about ¼ inch thick
3 medium-sized onions, sliced about ¼ inch thick

In a large deep skillet, heat the oil over medium heat. Brown the steak for 2 minutes per side. Add the tomato sauce, water, allspice, salt, and pepper. Cover and reduce the heat to low; simmer for 30 to 35 minutes. Add the remaining ingredients and simmer for 45 more minutes, or until the potatoes are cooked through and the meat is fork-tender. Slice the meat and serve with the veggies and pan juices.

NOTE: Some butchers call this cut a chuck steak, while others refer to it as a chuck roast, so don't be confused. No matter what it's called, it'll still have that lip-smacking goodness.

FOR A LEANER FINISHED DISH,
TRIM EXCESS FAT BEFORE COOKING

Apricot Brisket

* * *

4 to 6 servings

How rare it is to find fresh apricots in the supermarket. There are two reasons for that: one, because they have such a short season, and two, because when they *are* in season, they disappear in *no* time! Well, now you can enjoy that great apricot taste all year-round. Oh, just like fresh apricots, this dish will disappear before you know it!

    1 jar (10 ounces) apricot preserves (about ¾ cup)
    1 envelope (1 ounce) onion soup mix
    1 cup ketchup
    1 cup dry red wine
    One 2½- to 3-pound beef brisket

Preheat the oven to 350°F. In a medium-sized bowl, combine the apricot preserves, onion soup mix, ketchup, and wine. Place the brisket in a 9" × 13" baking dish that has been coated with nonstick vegetable spray. Spread the apricot mixture over the brisket and cover tightly with aluminum foil. Bake for 2½ to 3 hours, or until fork-tender. Slice across the grain and serve with the sauce.

NOTE: For an even fruitier taste, I like to add a drained 17-ounce can of apricot halves during the last 30 minutes of cooking.

USE OR FREEZE LEFTOVERS AS SOON AS POSSIBLE

Garlic Roast

* * *

6 to 8 servings

Too often a roast has loads of flavor on the outside, and none in the center. Not this one! It's got something different...the center is stuffed with roasted garlic.

One 3- to 3½-pound beef eye of the round roast
1 tablespoon plus 2 teaspoons vegetable oil, divided
8 to 10 whole garlic cloves, peeled
1 teaspoon paprika
½ teaspoon onion powder
¾ teaspoon salt
½ teaspoon black pepper

Preheat the oven to 350°F. Using a long, thin knife, carefully make a horizontal slit through the center of the roast. Twist the knife gently to make a ½-inch hole. (The hole doesn't have to stay open on its own because it's going to be stuffed with garlic.) In a small saucepan, heat the 2 teaspoons of oil over medium-high heat. Sauté the garlic cloves for 3 to 4 minutes, until lightly browned, stirring often. Remove from the heat and allow to cool. In a small bowl, combine the remaining ingredients; mix well and set aside. When the garlic is cool enough to handle, push the cloves into the hole in the center of the roast until they fill the hole. Rub the oil mixture over the entire roast and place in a 7" × 11" baking dish. Roast for 1 to 1¼ hours or until a meat thermometer inserted in the center registers 160°F. for medium, or cook until desired doneness beyond that.

Salted Eye of the Round Barbecue

* * *

8 to 10 servings

I included this one because it's one of my most requested meat recipes, even though it has to be done outdoors. It's made directly on barbecue coals or on the lava rocks of a gas grill. (*You need to follow the directions carefully and give it your complete attention.*)

> One 4- to 5-pound beef eye of the round roast, trimmed
> 4 cups kosher (coarse) salt

Remove the grate from your grill, then preheat the grill to high heat. (With a charcoal grill, this means letting the fire go until there is a good bed of red-hot coals.) Meanwhile, tear off a piece of waxed paper large enough to wrap the roast completely. (Use two sheets if necessary, and overlap them.) Place the waxed paper flat on a countertop, place the roast in the center, and pour the kosher salt over the meat. Use your clean hands to spread the salt evenly all over the meat, until it is completely covered and white. **Do not be afraid to use too much salt.** Wrap the meat with the waxed paper as completely as you can, so that all of the salt stays inside the wrapper. Here's where you need to be careful: Place the waxed paper–wrapped meat directly on the hot coals or lava rocks and stand back immediately because the waxed paper will instantly flame up and burn away. Leave the grill cover off. Let the meat cook for 35 to 40 minutes on one side. Then use two long-handled meat forks or long-handled tongs to flip the meat, and cook it for 30 to 35 minutes more on the second side. Again, **do not cover the grill.** Carefully remove the meat from the coals and scrape off any remaining bits of waxed paper and salt. (The outside of the meat will be black.) Place the meat in something shallow for carving, so that the juices can be saved for serving over it. Carve the roast across the grain in thin (about ¼-inch) slices.

NOTE: If you follow the directions carefully, you'll end up with a range of slices from medium-rare to well-done, so that everybody can have moist and delicious roast beef done their own perfect way. **Please be sure to keep children away from your fire.**

Lemon Herb "Roast"

* * *

6 to 8 servings

Oven-roasting gives this a moist, tender texture while slowly cooking the vegetables. And broiling it to finish it up gives the meat a crisp, zesty flavor. Yup, here's the way for us to get the best of both worlds!

One 3- to 3½-pound boneless beef top sirloin steak, about 2 inches thick
½ cup chopped fresh parsley
2 tablespoons olive oil
4 garlic cloves, minced
2 teaspoons grated fresh lemon peel
3 tablespoons lemon juice
1 teaspoon salt
½ teaspoon black pepper
3 medium-sized white potatoes, cut into 1-inch chunks
3 medium-sized carrots, cut into ½-inch chunks
2 medium-sized onions, cut into quarters

Preheat the oven to 400°F. Place the steak in a roasting pan that has been coated with nonstick vegetable spray. In a large bowl, combine the parsley, olive oil, garlic, lemon peel, lemon juice, salt, and pepper; mix well and rub half of the mixture onto the top and sides of the steak. Add the potatoes, carrots, and onions to the remaining lemon mixture; toss until the vegetables are well coated, then place them around the steak in the roasting pan. Cover and roast for 50 to 60 minutes for medium (160°F. on a meat thermometer), or until desired doneness, stirring the vegetables occasionally. Remove the cover and broil in a preheated broiler for 5 to 6 minutes, or until the top is browned. Slice across the grain and serve with the vegetables and pan juices.

Cola Roast

* * *

8 to 10 servings

Cola on a *roast*?! You're probably thinking that it sounds crazy, but after one bite you'll know it's *not*. I happen to think the taste is (can I say it?) awesome!

1 teaspoon salt
1/2 teaspoon black pepper
1/2 teaspoon garlic powder
One 4- to 5-pound beef bottom round roast
3 tablespoons vegetable oil
1 can (12 ounces) carbonated cola beverage
1 bottle (12 ounces) chili sauce
2 tablespoons Worcestershire sauce
2 tablespoons hot pepper sauce

> FOR A LEANER FINISHED DISH,
> TRIM EXCESS FAT BEFORE COOKING

Preheat the oven to 325°F. In a small bowl, combine the salt, pepper, and garlic powder; mix well and rub over the surface of the roast. In a soup pot, heat the oil over medium-high heat and brown the roast on all sides. Transfer the roast to a roasting pan that has been coated with nonstick vegetable spray. In a medium-sized bowl, combine the remaining ingredients; mix well and pour over the roast. Cover with aluminum foil and roast for 2 1/2 to 3 hours, or until the meat is fork-tender.

NOTE: Any kind of cola works just fine—regular, diet, or caffeine-free—the choice is yours.

Raspberry-Glazed Corned Beef

* * *

12 to 15 servings

This is a little different, with a lot of flavor. It's got just the right balance of sweet and spicy.

One 4- to 4½-pound cooked corned beef
1 cup raspberry preserves
2 teaspoons lime juice
1 teaspoon hot pepper sauce

Preheat the oven to 350°F. Place the corned beef in a large roasting pan that has been coated with nonstick vegetable spray. In a small bowl, combine the remaining ingredients. Spread evenly over the corned beef. Cover tightly with aluminum foil and bake for 2 to 2½ hours, until the corned beef is fork-tender. Baste with the pan juices several times during cooking and uncover for the final 20 minutes. Slice across the grain in thin slices and serve with the pan juices.

NOTE: If you've got any corned beef left over, slice it thin for really tasty sandwiches.

So-Tender Short Ribs

* * *

4 to 6 servings

My grandfather used to use that favorite expression "Good things come to those who wait." Well, here's the proof that it's true!

3 to 4 pounds beef short ribs
1 large onion, cut into chunks
2 medium-sized red bell peppers, cut into ½-inch strips
1 cup barbecue sauce
1 cup ready-to-use beef broth
½ teaspoon salt
½ teaspoon black pepper
½ cup water
¼ cup all-purpose flour

Preheat the oven to 350°F. In a large nonstick skillet, brown the ribs over medium-high heat for 6 to 7 minutes, turning to brown all sides. Drain off the excess liquid and place the ribs in a 9" × 13" baking dish that has been coated with nonstick vegetable spray. Cover the ribs with the onion and bell peppers. In a medium-sized bowl, combine the barbecue sauce, broth, salt, and black pepper; mix well and pour over the ribs and vegetables. Cover tightly with aluminum foil and bake for 1 to 1¼ hours, or until the meat is just fork-tender. In a small bowl, whisk together the water and flour until smooth. Pour the flour mixture into the pan drippings and mix with a fork or whisk. Cover tightly with aluminum foil and return to the oven for 30 minutes, or until the meat is very tender and the sauce is thickened.

Peaches Foster Glazed Ham

* * *

10 to 12 servings

In the past I've shared my recipes for Bananas Foster and Bananas Foster Crunch Cake. What knockout desserts! Now it's time for me to share this spin-off recipe that slow-bakes ham with peaches and those same rich flavors for a real knockout main course.

One 6- to 7-pound fully cooked ham
1/4 cup (1/2 stick) butter
1 cup firmly packed dark brown sugar
2 cans (16 ounces each) sliced peaches, drained and cut into 1/2-inch
    chunks

Preheat the oven to 325°F. Place the ham in a roasting pan that has been coated with nonstick vegetable spray and bake for 1 hour. In a medium-sized skillet, melt the butter and brown sugar over medium heat until well mixed and almost caramelized. Stir in the peaches; mix well. Remove the ham from the oven and pour the glaze over the entire ham. Bake for 25 to 30 more minutes. Remove the ham from the pan and place on a serving platter. Carve at the table and serve with the warm glaze from the pan.

NOTE: Sliced thin, the leftovers make great sandwiches. If you'd like your sauce to be sweet and spicy, add 1 teaspoon hot pepper sauce when you add the peaches.

USE OR FREEZE LEFTOVERS AS SOON AS POSSIBLE

Shortcut Pork Sauerbraten

* * *

4 to 6 servings

Did you know that traditional beef-style sauerbraten marinates for days? Well, with this shortcut pork version we can go from start to finish in only $1^1/_2$ hours!

2 tablespoons olive oil, divided
2 medium-sized onions, halved and sliced very thin
$^1/_4$ pound thinly sliced deli ham, cut into $^1/_2$-inch strips
8 cups shredded Chinese cabbage or Salad Savoy
2 tablespoons balsamic vinegar
One $1^1/_2$- to 2-pound boneless center-cut single pork loin
$^1/_2$ teaspoon paprika
$^1/_2$ teaspoon garlic powder

In a soup pot, heat 1 tablespoon oil over medium heat. Add the onions and ham and cook for 10 to 12 minutes, until the onions are browned, stirring occasionally. Add the cabbage and balsamic vinegar and cook for 10 minutes. Meanwhile, coat the pork loin with the remaining oil and the paprika and garlic powder. Reduce the heat to low and place the pork loin over the cabbage. Cover and simmer for 1 to $1^1/_4$ hours, or until the pork is cooked through. Cut into thin slices and serve topped with the cooked cabbage mixture.

STORE MEAT COVERED IN THE REFRIGERATOR BETWEEN 35°F. AND 40°F.

Glazed Leg of Lamb

* * *

10 to 12 servings

You can really fool your dinner crowd with this one. You know, 'cause it looks so fancy, but it's so easy to make. And the taste...well, decide for yourself.

One 7- to 9-pound leg of lamb
1 teaspoon salt
1/2 teaspoon black pepper
1/2 cup grape jelly
1/2 cup ketchup
1/2 cup dry red wine
1 teaspoon dried oregano

Preheat the oven to 350°F. Sprinkle the lamb all over with the salt and pepper and place on a roasting rack that has been coated with non-stick vegetable spray. Place the rack in a large roasting pan filled with 1/4 inch of water. Roast the lamb for 30 minutes. In a small saucepan, combine the remaining ingredients and heat over low heat until the jelly melts, stirring occasionally. Brush the lamb with the mixture. Roast the lamb for 3 to 3 1/2 hours more, or until a meat thermometer registers 160°F. for medium, or until desired doneness beyond that, brushing the lamb every 30 minutes with some of the remaining jelly mixture. Bring the remaining jelly mixture to a boil, then serve with the lamb.

Crown Roast of Lamb

* * *

4 servings

Kings and queens aren't the only ones who can have crowns...uh-uh! When you serve this crown roast of lamb, your family and guests will surely feel like royalty!

One 2- to 2½-pound crown roast of lamb
1 tablespoon peanut oil
1½ teaspoons salt, divided
½ teaspoon black pepper
1½ cups cooked rice
5 ounces fresh mushrooms, sliced (about 2 cups)
¼ teaspoon chopped fresh parsley
2 tablespoons butter, melted

Preheat the oven to 325°F. Place the crown roast in a shallow roasting pan that has been coated with nonstick vegetable spray. In a small bowl, combine the oil, 1 teaspoon salt, and the pepper; mix well. Rub the mixture over the entire roast. In a medium-sized bowl, combine the rice, remaining salt, mushrooms, parsley, and butter; mix well. Fill the cavity of the roast with the rice stuffing. Protect the ends of the rib bones from overbrowning by wrapping each of them in aluminum foil. Roast, uncovered, for 1 to 1¼ hours, until a meat thermometer registers 160°F. for medium, or until desired doneness beyond that. Transfer the roast to a serving platter and allow to stand for 15 to 20 minutes to firm up before slicing between the bones.

NOTE: You can find a crown roast of lamb at the meat counter, or ask the butcher to prepare it for you. Before serving, be sure to discard any string that may have been used by the butcher to tie the roast together.

Minestrone Lamb Shanks

* * *

4 servings

You can't miss with these plump, tender lamb shanks combined with a hearty minestrone taste and a sauce that's perfect for dunking. (Don't forget the crusty bread!)

    2 tablespoons vegetable oil
    4 lamb shanks (10 to 12 ounces each)
    1 can (19 ounces) minestrone soup
    1 can (10$\frac{1}{2}$ ounces) condensed beef broth
    1 can (14$\frac{1}{2}$ ounces) stewed tomatoes
    1 teaspoon ground cumin
    1 teaspoon garlic powder
    1 teaspoon onion powder
    $\frac{1}{2}$ teaspoon salt
    $\frac{1}{2}$ teaspoon black pepper
    $\frac{3}{4}$ cup instant mashed potato flakes

In a large skillet, heat the oil over medium heat. Brown the lamb shanks, turning occasionally, for 15 to 20 minutes, or until evenly browned. In a large bowl, combine the remaining ingredients except the potato flakes; mix well. Pour over the browned shanks. Bring to a boil, then reduce the heat to low, cover, and simmer for 2 to 2$\frac{1}{2}$ hours, or until the shanks are fork-tender. Remove the shanks to a serving platter. Add the potato flakes to the pan juices; mix well and simmer for 3 to 4 minutes, or until thickened. Return the shanks to the skillet and coat with the sauce.

Showstopping Stuffed Veal

* * *

4 servings

This weekend, why not give your gang a treat—a stuffed veal breast! It's a tasty centerpiece for your dinner table . . . a true showstopper!

One 4½- to 5½-pound breast of veal, with pocket for stuffing (see Note)
2 tablespoons butter
1 medium-sized zucchini, coarsely grated (about 2 cups)
1 package (6 ounces) instant stuffing mix
2 tablespoons vegetable oil
½ teaspoon salt
½ teaspoon black pepper
½ teaspoon onion powder
½ teaspoon garlic powder
½ teaspoon ground dried thyme
1 teaspoon paprika

Preheat the oven to 350°F. Place the veal breast into a large roasting pan that has been coated with nonstick vegetable spray. In a large skillet, melt the butter over medium-high heat and sauté the zucchini for 6 to 7 minutes, or until tender. Prepare the stuffing mix according to the package directions. Add the zucchini to the stuffing; mix well. Spoon the stuffing mixture into the pocket of the veal breast; do not pack tightly. If any stuffing remains, bake separately in a small covered baking dish. In a small bowl, combine the remaining ingredi-

ents. Brush the spice mixture evenly over the top of the veal and bake uncovered for 2 to 2½ hours, or until the juices run clear and the meat is fork-tender.

NOTE: Cutting a pocket into the veal breast is easy, but it's even easier for us when we ask the butcher to do it!

Soups, Salads, and Sandwiches

By now you must have cooked up some great meals using lots of different meat cuts, from ground meat to steaks to roasts. Okay, it's time to use those same meats in a lighter way—highlighting all-new soups, salads, and sandwiches.

Even though a number of these recipes call for meats from the deli or the meat department, most can be made with leftovers. We can turn your leftover roast into Beefy Barley Soup (page 178), and that holiday ham can become Honey-Mustard Pork Salad (page 190). These are super ways to make a small amount of meat go a long way. Whether you want to start from scratch, or whip your leftovers into brand-new treats (and nobody would ever know!), these are creative, meaty ways to enjoy your soups, salads, and sandwiches. And here are some ways to give your leftovers a new life and other foods an extra boost:

- Add lean leftover meat to canned soups to give them a rich, homemade flavor.
- Cut up small cooked pieces of meat (or cook raw ones if you have them) for adding to pasta and vegetable salads.

- Finely chop leftover cooked meats and mix with mayonnaise to make quick sandwich spreads.
- Turn thinly sliced roast beef into sandwich favorites like Philadelphia Cheese Steak Sandwiches (page 194) or French Double Dippers (page 191).

Soups, Salads, and Sandwiches

Beefy Barley Soup

* * *

4 to 6 servings

Want to share that warm, cozy feeling at your kitchen table? This recipe's for you! It's a satisfying meal by itself. What are you waiting for? Get cookin'!

8 cups water
2 cans (10½ ounces each) condensed beef broth
¾ to 1 pound beef top round, cut into ½-inch cubes
2 large onions, chopped
1 pound fresh mushrooms, sliced
4 medium-sized carrots, sliced
2 large celery stalks, chopped
1½ teaspoons salt
½ teaspoon black pepper
1 cup barley

In a soup pot, combine all of the ingredients except the barley; bring to a boil over medium-high heat. Reduce the heat to low and simmer for 30 minutes, stirring occasionally. Add the barley and continue to simmer for 1½ to 2 more hours, until the barley is tender.

NOTE: If you have a little leftover pot roast or steak, just cut it up and use it instead of the top round. And if you use meat that's already cooked, the cooking time for the soup can be reduced a little—just make sure the barley is cooked until tender.

"Souper" Burger Soup

* * *

10 to 14 servings

We've all had barbecue parties where we made a few too many burgers, and then they ended up sitting in the fridge for days before finally being thrown out. Well, that won't happen anymore 'cause here's a great way to enjoy them a second time—and the buns, too!

Four ¼-pound cold cooked hamburgers, broken into large chunks
½ teaspoon salt
½ teaspoon black pepper
2 cans (14½ ounces each) ready-to-use beef broth
1 can (28 ounces) crushed tomatoes
1 medium-sized onion, chopped
¼ cup sweet relish
2 tablespoons ketchup
1 tablespoon prepared yellow mustard
2 hamburger buns, torn or cut into 2-inch pieces

In a soup pot, combine all the ingredients except the buns. Bring to a boil over medium-high heat, then reduce the heat to medium-low. Simmer for 20 to 25 minutes, or until the onions are tender. Add the buns and cook for an additional 8 to 10 minutes, stirring frequently, or until the buns dissolve and the soup thickens.

NOTE: If you don't have leftover cooked hamburgers, you can sauté 1 pound ground beef until no pink remains, drain it, and add it in place of the cooked hamburgers.

ALWAYS COOK
GROUND MEAT UNTIL
WELL-DONE
NO PINK REMAINS AND
THE JUICES RUN CLEAR

Beef Vegetable Soup

* * *

4 to 6 servings

Here's an all-time classic that's good anytime, but especially on a chilly autumn day. With some crusty bread and a salad, you've got a whole meal. And the best part is, you can use your leftover meats in place of the top round.

> 1 to 1¼ pounds beef top round or boneless top sirloin steak, cut into
> ½-inch cubes
> 1 can (14½ ounces) ready-to-use beef broth
> 1 can (28 ounces) crushed tomatoes
> 1 teaspoon Italian seasoning
> ¾ teaspoon salt
> ¼ teaspoon black pepper
> ⅛ teaspoon cayenne pepper
> 2 packages (16 ounces each) frozen mixed vegetables

In a large saucepan, combine all of the ingredients and bring to a boil over medium-high heat. Reduce the heat to low, cover, and simmer for 20 to 25 minutes, or until the meat is tender.

NOTE: Any kind of mixed vegetables will work, and because there are so many different blends to choose from, that makes it even easier to include everyone's favorites.

> FOR A LEANER FINISHED DISH,
> TRIM EXCESS FAT BEFORE COOKING

Quick Steak Soup

* * *

4 to 6 servings

You're saying, "This must be a misprint. Steak *soup*?! No way!" Well, it's right. Read on so I can show you how to have your favorite steak taste served up in a soup. It's easy to make and even easier to eat. I guess that means it's easy to be a kitchen hero!

1 pound boneless beef top sirloin steak, 1 inch thick
3 cans (14½ ounces each) ready-to-use beef broth
1 package (10 ounces) frozen whole pearl onions
1 package (9 ounces) frozen baby carrots, thawed and drained
1 package (9 ounces) frozen French-cut green beans, thawed and
   drained
⅛ teaspoon ground dried thyme
¼ teaspoon black pepper
1 tablespoon steak sauce

Cut the steak into ¼" × 1" slices. Place in a soup pot and add the remaining ingredients. Bring to a boil over high heat. Cover, reduce the heat to low, and simmer for 45 to 50 minutes to allow the flavors to "marry."

NOTE: Any type of leftover steak will work in this recipe. And it's even better if the steak has already been seasoned or topped with steak sauce. Just slice it thin and use it as above.

STORE MEAT COVERED IN THE REFRIGERATOR BETWEEN 35°F. AND 40°F.

Lemony Lamb Soup

* * *

6 to 8 servings

In just about an hour, you can have a big pot of some of the best homemade soup you've ever eaten. Be careful—you may become a soupaholic after trying this!

1½ to 2 pounds lamb stew meat or boneless leg of lamb, cut into
    ½-inch chunks
2 medium-sized onions, chopped
2 large stalks celery, chopped
2 medium-sized carrots, coarsely chopped
2 cans (14½ ounces each) ready-to-use chicken broth
2 cups water
¼ teaspoon dried rosemary
½ teaspoon dried thyme
1 teaspoon dried dill
1 teaspoon salt
½ teaspoon black pepper
½ cup uncooked orzo or Rosamarina pasta
3 eggs
⅓ cup lemon juice
1 package (10 ounces) frozen chopped spinach, thawed and drained

ALWAYS CHECK THE "SELL BY" DATE ON MEAT PACKAGES

In a soup pot, combine the lamb, onions, celery, carrots, broth, water, rosemary, thyme, dill, salt, and pepper. Bring to a boil, then reduce the heat to low and simmer, covered, for 30 minutes. Increase the heat to medium and add the orzo. Cook, uncovered, for 10 to 12 minutes, or until the orzo is tender. Meanwhile, in a medium-sized bowl, beat together the eggs and lemon juice. Remove 1 cup of the hot broth from the soup pot and slowly whisk into the egg mixture. When the orzo is cooked, reduce the heat to low and whisk the egg mixture slowly into the soup pot. Add the spinach and cook for 5 to 10 more minutes, or until the soup is slightly thickened. Serve immediately.

NOTE: If you have some leftover cooked leg of lamb and don't know what to do with it, this is the perfect way to make a second meal with it. And with the lemon and egg in here, the lamb will have a whole new taste.

Easy Wonton Soup

* * *

4 to 6 servings

Never tried making wonton soup at home? It's not difficult, if that's what you thought. Actually, this version is simple as 1–2–3.

- 1 to 1¼ pounds ground pork
- ½ teaspoon ground ginger
- ½ teaspoon black pepper
- 3 cans (14½ ounces each) ready-to-use chicken broth
- 1 cup water
- 2 tablespoons soy sauce
- 2½ ounces fresh mushrooms, sliced (1 cup)
- 6 scallions, sliced
- 1 package (6 ounces) wonton skins, cut into ½-inch strips

In a soup pot, brown the pork over medium-high heat for 3 to 5 minutes, or until no pink remains. Drain off the excess liquid. Reduce the heat to medium and add the remaining ingredients except the wonton skins; bring to a boil. Separate the wonton strips and stir into the soup. Cook for 8 to 10 more minutes, or until the wontons are cooked.

ALWAYS COOK
GROUND MEAT UNTIL
WELL-DONE:
NO PINK REMAINS AND
THE JUICES RUN CLEAR

Almost Gumbo

* * *

4 to 6 servings

Smoked sausage, okra . . . just talking about it makes me taste all the exciting New Orleans flavors of Creole and Cajun cooking. With this hearty recipe you can share the tastes, too—in less than 30 minutes!

3/4 to 1 pound smoked beef sausage, cut in half lengthwise, then into
  1/2-inch slices
4 cups water
1 can (14 1/2 ounces) stewed tomatoes
1 package (10 ounces) frozen cut okra, thawed and drained
2 teaspoons dried thyme
1 teaspoon garlic powder
1/2 cup long-grain rice
1/4 cup dry red wine
1 tablespoon hot pepper sauce

In a soup pot, combine the sausage, water, tomatoes, okra, thyme, and garlic powder. Bring to a boil over medium heat, then reduce the heat to low and add the remaining ingredients. Simmer for 20 to 25 minutes, or until the rice is cooked, stirring occasionally.

NOTE: If you don't like smoked sausage, you can substitute sweet or hot Italian sausage. Just brown it, then follow the directions above.

Beefy Summer Salad

* * *

4 to 5 servings

Why not turn leftover roast beef into a refreshing main dish salad? It's great in *any* season!

3/4 to 1 pound cooked roast beef, cut into 1/2-inch cubes
1 medium-sized tomato, coarsely chopped
1 medium-sized cucumber, peeled, seeded, and coarsely chopped
1/2 head iceberg lettuce, coarsely chopped
1/2 cup mayonnaise
1 teaspoon onion powder
1/2 teaspoon dried dill
1/4 teaspoon salt
1 teaspoon black pepper

In a large bowl, combine the roast beef, tomato, cucumber, and lettuce; set aside. In a small bowl, combine the remaining ingredients to make a dressing. Pour over the lettuce mixture and toss to coat. Cover and refrigerate for 1 to 2 hours before serving.

NOTE: Any kind of roast beef will do. You can ask for a few 1/2-inch-thick pieces of roast beef at the deli.

Hot and Cold Pasta Salad

* * *

4 to 6 servings

Chilled pasta tossed with warm beef and broccoli stir-fry is just what you need when you're looking for a change from traditional pasta salads.

> ½ cup Italian dressing, divided
> ½ cup plus 1 tablespoon soy sauce, divided
> 3 garlic cloves, minced
> ½ teaspoon ground ginger
> ½ cup orange juice
> 1 to 1¼ pounds beef flank steak, cut into ¼-inch strips
> 12 ounces uncooked bow tie noodles
> ½ teaspoon white pepper
> ½ head broccoli, cut into florets

ALWAYS DISCARD USED MARINADE

In a large bowl, combine 2 tablespoons Italian dressing, ½ cup soy sauce, garlic, ginger, and orange juice. Place the steak strips into the mixture; cover and chill for 1 to 2 hours. Meanwhile, cook the noodles according to the package directions; drain, rinse, and drain well. Set aside in a large bowl and allow to cool. In a small bowl, combine the pepper and the remaining Italian dressing and soy sauce. Coat a large skillet with nonstick vegetable spray and heat over medium-high heat; remove the beef from the marinade and add to the skillet, discarding the remaining marinade. Add the broccoli and stir-fry for 4 to 5 minutes, until the broccoli is crisp-tender. Add the beef and dressing mixtures to the noodles; toss until well mixed. Serve immediately.

Picnic Salad

* * *

4 to 5 servings

With this combination of potatoes and ham, you've got an all-in-one meal that's perfect to take along to a picnic in your backyard or at the park.

2 pounds cooked small red potatoes, cut into 1/2-inch cubes
1/4 cup mayonnaise
1 tablespoon honey
2 teaspoons vegetable oil
1 teaspoon white vinegar
2 teaspoons prepared yellow mustard
1 teaspoon black pepper
1/2 pound deli ham, sliced 1/2 inch thick, cubed
2 celery stalks, coarsely chopped

In a large bowl, combine all the ingredients; toss until the potatoes are coated. Cover and refrigerate for several hours, or until thoroughly chilled.

NOTE: What a great way to use leftover cooked ham! Just cut it up and toss it in.

Lickety-Split Pasta Salad

* * *

8 to 10 servings

This is the perfect recipe for "make-ahead" days—you know, those days when you know you're going to be too busy to cook dinner. Just make it the night before, or even in the morning!

    1 pound uncooked tricolor pasta spirals
    1 pound cooked roast beef, cut into ¼-inch cubes
    2 medium-sized tomatoes, chopped
    1 medium-sized green bell pepper, finely chopped
    1 medium-sized onion, finely chopped
    ¾ cup Italian dressing
    ½ cup mayonnaise
    ½ teaspoon black pepper

Cook the pasta according to the package directions; drain, rinse under cold water, and drain again. Place in a medium-sized bowl and allow to cool. Add the roast beef, tomatoes, green pepper, and onion; mix well. In a small bowl, combine the remaining ingredients; mix well, then pour over the pasta mixture and toss to coat. Cover and chill for at least 1 hour before serving.

NOTE: Any kind of leftover beef will work with this salad, or get some thick-sliced roast beef from the deli.

STORE MEAT COVERED IN THE REFRIGERATOR BETWEEN 35°F. AND 40°F.

Honey-Mustard Pork Salad

* * *

4 to 6 servings

You can make this salad with any leftover pork, or just stir-fry some fresh pork loin and you're ready to go!

    1 pound cooked pork, cut into ½-inch chunks (about 3 cups)
    ½ of a 10-ounce bag of spinach, washed and torn into bite-sized
        pieces
    2 medium-sized carrots, shredded
    1 medium-sized apple, peeled, cored, and chopped
    1 bottle (8 ounces) honey-mustard dressing

In a large salad bowl, combine all of the ingredients; toss to coat.

NOTE: For extra crunchiness, sprinkle 2 tablespoons chopped peanuts over the top of the salad.

French Double Dippers

∗ ∗ ∗

6 sandwiches

I call these double dippers 'cause you warm the beef in the broth, then serve the broth along with the sandwiches for dipping. Yes, yes, they're double delicious.

    1 can (14½ ounces) ready-to-use beef broth
    ½ teaspoon black pepper
    ½ teaspoon garlic powder
    ½ teaspoon onion powder
    2 pounds thinly sliced roast beef
    6 hoagie or hard rolls, split

In a large skillet, combine the broth, pepper, garlic powder, and onion powder. Warm over medium heat just until boiling and stir in the roast beef. Cook for 3 to 4 minutes, or until the beef is heated through. Use tongs to place the beef evenly over the rolls and serve with individual bowls of the broth mixture for dipping.

NOTE: Instead of using roast beef from the deli, you can make it yourself. Old-fashioned Deli Roast Beef (page 157) is a quick and easy way to make great-tasting roast beef.

STORE MEAT COVERED IN THE REFRIGERATOR BETWEEN 35°F. AND 40°F.

South-of-the-Border Steak Sandwiches

* * *

3 to 6 servings

This is a South-of-the-Border version of a Philly cheese steak sandwich. That means it's got that great Mexican spiciness!

1 tablespoon vegetable oil
1 medium-sized onion, cut into ¼-inch wedges
1 to 1½ pounds boneless beef top sirloin steak, cut into short, thin strips
¾ cup medium picante sauce
1 teaspoon ground cumin
¾ teaspoon garlic powder, or to taste
Three 8-inch hoagie or hero rolls, split
1 cup (4 ounces) shredded Monterey Jack cheese

FOR A LEANER FINISHED DISH, TRIM EXCESS FAT BEFORE COOKING

In a large skillet, heat the oil over medium-high heat. Add the onion and sauté for 3 minutes, stirring frequently. Add the steak and cook for 4 to 5 minutes, or until the steak is no longer pink. Add the picante sauce, cumin, and garlic powder. Increase the heat to high and cook, stirring constantly, for 2 more minutes, or until most of the liquid has evaporated. Preheat the broiler. Place the rolls cut side up on a cookie sheet and broil just until golden. Spoon the meat mixture evenly over the rolls and top with the cheese. Broil for 3 to 5 minutes, or just until the cheese has melted. Cut the sandwiches in half and serve with additional picante sauce, if desired.

NOTE: If you like Cheddar cheese, why not try a Tex-Mex cheese blend instead of just the Monterey Jack? And if you're starting with leftover steak, just cut it into thin strips, add it to the skillet with the picante sauce and continue as directed from there.

Meatball Hoagies

* * *

6 sandwiches

Hoagies, heroes, or submarines...what you call these depends on what part of the country you're from. But whatever you call them, they sure are tasty sandwiches!

1 1/2 pounds ground beef
1/3 cup dry bread crumbs
1/3 cup grated Parmesan cheese
1 egg
3/4 teaspoon garlic powder
3/4 teaspoon salt
1/2 teaspoon black pepper
2 jars (28 ounces each) spaghetti sauce
6 hoagie rolls, split

In a large bowl, combine all the ingredients except the spaghetti sauce and the rolls; mix well. Form the beef mixture into eighteen 1 1/2-inch meatballs and place in a soup pot. Add the spaghetti sauce and stir gently to mix. Bring to a boil over medium heat, then reduce the heat to low, cover loosely, and simmer for 25 to 30 minutes, or until the meatballs are cooked through. Spoon 3 meatballs and some sauce onto each roll and serve.

NOTE: The meatballs and sauce can also be used for topping spaghetti. And you can use the meatballs in a soup or stew, too.

Philadelphia Cheese Steak Sandwiches

* * *

4 sandwiches

I love it when my travels take me to the home of the Philadelphia Cheese Steak Sandwich. Aside from meeting all of you, that's the best part of traveling!

3 tablespoons vegetable oil
2 large onions, thinly sliced
1 to 1¼ pounds thinly sliced roast beef
½ teaspoon salt
¼ teaspoon black pepper
4 hoagie rolls, split
4 slices (4 ounces total) provolone cheese

Preheat the oven to 350°F. In a large skillet, heat the oil over medium-high heat. Add the onions and sauté for 5 to 7 minutes, or until tender and lightly browned. Add the roast beef, salt, and pepper. Sauté for 3 to 4 minutes, or until the beef is completely heated through. Use tongs to place the meat mixture evenly over the roll bottoms. Place the open sandwiches on a large cookie sheet and place 1 slice of cheese over the meat. Bake for 3 to 4 minutes, or until the cheese has melted. Cover with the tops of the rolls and serve immediately.

NOTE: If you want to have the roast beef for these great-tasting sandwiches always on hand, make Old-fashioned Deli Roast Beef (page 157), then slice, wrap, and freeze it.

Saucy Pork Sandwiches

* * *

4 sandwiches

Regular ham sandwiches are good, but here's a way to have pork sandwiches that are a step above the rest. Yup, with the tomato sauce and bell peppers, these have got a saucy new taste you're gonna love.

3 tablespoons vegetable oil, divided
1 pound boneless pork loin, trimmed and cut into 1-inch cubes
1 medium-sized onion, chopped
1 medium-sized green bell pepper, chopped
2 garlic cloves, chopped
1 can (8 ounces) tomato sauce
1 teaspoon chili powder
3/4 teaspoon salt
1/2 teaspoon black pepper
4 sandwich buns, split

> FOR A LEANER FINISHED DISH,
> TRIM EXCESS FAT BEFORE COOKING

In a large skillet, heat 1 tablespoon oil over medium-high heat. Add the pork and sauté for 3 to 5 minutes, or until no pink remains, stirring occasionally. With a slotted spoon, remove the meat from the skillet to the bowl of a food processor that is fitted with a cutting blade. Process until the meat is finely chopped; set aside. Add the remaining oil to the skillet and sauté the onion, green pepper, and garlic over medium-high heat for 4 to 5 minutes, or until the vegetables are tender. Add the chopped pork and the remaining ingredients except the buns. Reduce the heat to low, cover, and simmer for 5 to 10 minutes, or until heated through. Serve on the sandwich buns.

NOTE: This is perfect for any leftover pork: chops, ribs, or roast. Just remove the meat from the bone, finely chop it in a food processor, and follow the directions above. You can make a whole new meal!

Ham and Cheese Melts

* * *

8 sandwiches

These sandwiches are great for the kids to help put together because you get to wrap 'em, bake 'em, and unwrap 'em.

3/4 pound cooked ham, coarsely chopped
1 cup (4 ounces) shredded Cheddar cheese
1/2 cup medium salsa
6 scallions, sliced
8 hot dog buns

Preheat the oven to 350°F. In a medium-sized bowl, combine all of the ingredients except the hot dog buns; mix well. Spread the mixture evenly over the hot dog buns. Place each filled bun in the center of a 12" × 12" sheet of aluminum foil. Fold the edges together and twist the ends closed. Place the foil-wrapped buns on a large cookie sheet and bake for 20 minutes. Serve hot right from the oven.

NOTE: This is a great way to use leftover ham, but if you don't have any, you can always buy sliced deli ham and coarsely chop it. It works just as well.

Index

* * *

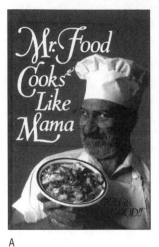

A

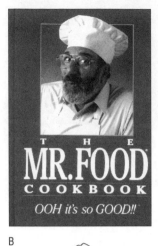

B

C

D

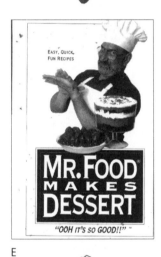

E

F

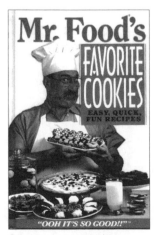

G

H

I

Mr. Food®'s Library Gives You More Ways to Say...
"OOH IT'S SO GOOD!!™"

WILLIAM MORROW

Mr. Food's Fun Kitchen Tips and Shortcuts (and Recipes, Too!)

J

Mr. Food's Old World Cooking Made Easy

K

"Help, Mr. Food! Company's Coming!" "OOH IT'S SO GOOD!™

L

Mr. Food Pizza 1-2-3

More than one million copies of Mr. Food® cookbooks sold!

M

Mr. Food Meat Around the Table

More than one million copies of Mr. Food® cookbooks sold!

N

Mr. Food Simply CHOCOLATE

More than one million copies of Mr. Food cookbooks sold!

O

Mr. Food®

Can Help You Be A Kitchen Hero!

Let Mr. Food® make your life easier with
Quick, No-Fuss Recipes and Helpful Kitchen Tips for

Family Dinners • Soups and Salads • Potluck Dishes
Barbecues • Special Brunches • Unbelievable Desserts

. . . and that's just the beginning!

Complete your **Mr. Food®** cookbook library today.
It's so simple to share in all the
"OOH IT'S SO GOOD!!"™

✂ -

TITLE	PRICE	QUANTITY	
A. **Mr. Food®** Cooks Like Mama	@ $12.95 each	x _____	= $_____
B. The **Mr. Food®** Cookbook, *OOH IT'S SO GOOD!!*™	@ $12.95 each	x _____	= $_____
C. **Mr. Food®** Cooks Chicken	@ $ 9.95 each	x _____	= $_____
D. **Mr. Food®** Cooks Pasta	@ $ 9.95 each	x _____	= $_____
E. **Mr. Food®** Makes Dessert	@ $ 9.95 each	x _____	= $_____
F. **Mr. Food®** Cooks Real American	@ $14.95 each	x _____	= $_____
G. **Mr. Food®'s** Favorite Cookies	@ $11.95 each	x _____	= $_____
H. **Mr. Food®'s** Quick and Easy Side Dishes	@ $11.95 each	x _____	= $_____
I. **Mr. Food®** Grills It All in a Snap	@ $11.95 each	x _____	= $_____
J. **Mr. Food®'s** Fun Kitchen Tips and Shortcuts (and Recipes, Too!)	@ $11.95 each	x _____	= $_____
K. **Mr. Food®'s** Old World Cooking Made Easy	@ $14.95 each	x _____	= $_____
L. "Help, **Mr. Food®**! Company's Coming!"	@ $14.95 each	x _____	= $_____
M. **Mr. Food®** Pizza 1-2-3	@ $12.00 each	x _____	= $_____
N. **Mr. Food®** Meat Around the Table	@ $12.00 each	x _____	= $_____
O. **Mr. Food®** Simply Chocolate	@ $12.00 each	x _____	= $_____

Call 1-800-619-FOOD (3663) or send payment to:
Mr. Food®
P.O. Box 696
Holmes, PA 19043

Name _____

Street _____ Apt._____

City _____ State_____ Zip_____

Method of Payment: ☐ Check or Money Order Enclosed

☐ Credit Card: ☐ Visa ☐ MasterCard Expiration Date _____

Signature _____

Book Total	$_____
+$2.95 Postage & Handling First Copy *AND* $1 Ea. Add'l. Copy (Canadian Orders Add Add'l. $2.00 *Per Copy*)	$_____
Subtotal	$_____
Less $1.00 per book if ordering 3 or more books with this order	$ –_____
Add Applicable Sales Tax (FL Residents Only)	$_____
Total in U.S. Funds	$_____

Account #: ☐ ☐ ☐ ☐ ☐ ☐ ☐ ☐ ☐ ☐ ☐ ☐ ☐ ☐ ☐ ☐

Please allow 4 to 6 weeks for delivery.

BKM1